MW00846194

Prolonged Exposure for PTSD in Intensive Outpatient Programs (PE-IOP)

 **THAT WORK**

Editor-In-Chief

David H. Barlow, PhD

Scientific Advisory Board

Anne Marie Albano, PhD

Gillian Butler, PhD

David M. Clark, PhD

Edna B. Foa, PhD

Paul J. Frick, PhD

Jack M. Gorman, MD

Kirk Heilbrun, PhD

Robert J. McMahon, PhD

Peter E. Nathan, PhD

Christine Maguth Nezu, PhD

Matthew K. Nock, PhD

Paul Salkovskis, PhD

Bonnie Spring, PhD

Gail Steketee, PhD

John R. Weisz, PhD

G. Terence Wilson, PhD

✔ TREATMENTS THAT WORK

Prolonged Exposure for PTSD in Intensive Outpatient Programs (PE-IOP)

THERAPIST GUIDE

SHEILA A. M. RAUCH

BARBARA O. ROTHBAUM

ERIN R. SMITH

EDNA B. FOA

OXFORD
UNIVERSITY PRESS

OXFORD
UNIVERSITY PRESS

Oxford University Press is a department of the University of Oxford. It furthers
the University's objective of excellence in research, scholarship, and education
by publishing worldwide. Oxford is a registered trade mark of Oxford University
Press in the UK and certain other countries.

Published in the United States of America by Oxford University Press
198 Madison Avenue, New York, NY 10016, United States of America.

© Oxford University Press 2020

All rights reserved. No part of this publication may be reproduced, stored in
a retrieval system, or transmitted, in any form or by any means, without the
prior permission in writing of Oxford University Press, or as expressly permitted
by law, by license, or under terms agreed with the appropriate reproduction
rights organization. Inquiries concerning reproduction outside the scope of the
above should be sent to the Rights Department, Oxford University Press, at the
address above.

You must not circulate this work in any other form
and you must impose this same condition on any acquirer.

Library of Congress Cataloging-in-Publication Data
Names: Rauch, Sheila A. M., author. | Rothbaum, Barbara O., author. |
Smith, Erin R. (Erin Regina), author. | Foa, Edna B., author.
Title: Prolonged exposure for PTSD in intensive outpatient programs (PE-IOP) /
Sheila A. M. Rauch, Barbara O. Rothbaum, Erin R. Smith, Edna B. Foa.
Description: New York, NY : Oxford University Press, [2020] |
Series: Treatments that work | Includes bibliographical references and index.
Identifiers: LCCN 2020006622 (print) | LCCN 2020006623 (ebook) |
ISBN 9780190081928 (paperback) | ISBN 9780190081942 (epub) |
ISBN 9780190081959
Subjects: LCSH: Post-traumatic stress disorder—Treatment. |
Cognitive therapy. | Psychiatric hospitals—Outpatient services.
Classification: LCC RC552.P67 R383 2020 (print) | LCC RC552.P67 (ebook) |
DDC 616.85/21—dc23
LC record available at https://lccn.loc.gov/2020006622
LC ebook record available at https://lccn.loc.gov/2020006623

9 8 7 6 5 4 3 2 1

Printed by Sheridan Books, Inc., United States of America

To all the trauma survivors I have known and worked with throughout my life. Your courage and dedication in the face of adversity inspires me and provides the fuel to constantly improve what I do.

To George, Nathan, and Edward. I love you and you keep me happy and energized.
—Sheila A. M. Rauch

With unending gratitude to the Wounded Warrior Project for challenging us to create an Intensive Outpatient Program and making it possible by funding it, to my colleagues at the Emory Healthcare Veterans Program who have created the best place in the world to be treated for PTSD, to our brave veterans and servicemen and servicewomen who serve for our freedom then face their demons when they come for treatment, and to my family, who make me feel like the luckiest person in the world.
—Barbara O. Rothbaum

To the veterans that I have had the honor to serve. To the veterans I have the honor to call my brother, sister, father, and grandfather. To the amazing VA staff that I have had the chance to serve alongside.

And lastly to Clay and Finnegan.
—Erin R. Smith

To my husband Charles and my daughters Yael and Michelle, who have always been supportive of my work even when it took me away from them, with much love and many thanks.
—Edna B. Foa

Stunning developments in healthcare have taken place over the past several years, but many of our widely accepted interventions and strategies in mental health and behavioral medicine have been brought into question by research evidence as not only lacking benefit, but perhaps inducing harm (Barlow, 2010). Other strategies have been proved effective using the best current standards of evidence, resulting in broad-based recommendations to make these practices more available to the public (McHugh & Barlow, 2010). Several recent developments are behind this revolution. First, we have arrived at a much deeper understanding of pathology, both psychological and physical, which has led to the development of new, more precisely targeted interventions. Second, our research methodologies have improved substantially, such that we have reduced threats to internal and external validity, thus making the outcomes more directly applicable to clinical situations. Third, governments around the world and healthcare systems and policymakers have decided that the quality of care should improve, that it should be evidence-based, and that it is in the public's interest to ensure that this happens (Barlow, 2004; Institute of Medicine, 2001, 2015; McHugh & Barlow, 2010).

Of course, the major stumbling block for clinicians everywhere is the accessibility of newly developed evidence-based psychological interventions. Workshops and books can go only so far in acquainting responsible and conscientious practitioners with the latest behavioral healthcare practices and their applicability to individual patients. This series, *Treatments ThatWork*™, is devoted to communicating these exciting new interventions to clinicians on the front lines of practice.

The manuals and workbooks in this series contain step-by-step detailed procedures for assessing and treating specific problems and diagnoses. But this series also goes beyond the books and manuals by providing ancillary materials that will approximate the supervisory process in assisting practitioners in the implementation of these procedures in their practice.

In our emerging healthcare system, the growing consensus is that evidence-based practice offers the most responsible course of action for the mental health professional. All behavioral healthcare clinicians deeply desire to provide the best possible care for their patients. In this series, our aim is to close the dissemination and information gap and make that possible.

This Guide addresses the treatment of posttraumatic stress disorder (PTSD) with a two-week prolonged exposure (PE) therapy protocol that combines individual and group formats and is designed to be implemented in an outpatient mental health setting. It is estimated that up to 83% of adults in the United States will experience a traumatic event at least once in their lives, with 20% of them going on to develop PTSD (Benjet et al., 2016). The guide is intended to be used by clinicians who are familiar with cognitive-behavioral therapy (CBT) generally and individual PE therapy specifically, as this format makes use of many of the components of individual PE. One of the greatest challenges in PTSD treatment is patients dropping out prior to completion. This PE-IOP manual addresses that challenge and achieves better than a 90% completion rate (Rauch et al., in press).

Because the processes and techniques presented here build on a treatment protocol with extensive empirical support accumulated over three decades, *Prolonged Exposure for Intensive Outpatient Programs (PE-IOP)* will be an indispensable resource for all practitioners who wish to effectively and efficiently help survivors of a range of traumatic experiences reduce symptoms and improve quality of life.

David H. Barlow, Editor-in-Chief
Treatments *That Work*™
Boston, Massachusetts

References

Barlow, D. H. (2004). Psychological treatments. *American Psychologist*, 59, 869–878.

Barlow, D. H. (2010). Negative effects from psychological treatments: A perspective. *American Psychologist*, 65(2), 13–20.

Benjet, C., Bromet, E., Karam, E. G., Kessler, R. C., McLaughlin, K. A., Ruscio, A. M., . . . Koenen, K. C. (2016). The epidemiology of traumatic event exposure worldwide: Results from the World Mental Health Survey Consortium. *Psychological Medicine*, 46(2), 327–343. doi:10.1017/S0033291715001981

Institute of Medicine (IOM). (2001). *Crossing the quality chasm: A new health system for the 21st century*. Washington, DC: National Academy Press.

Institute of Medicine (IOM). (2015). *Psychosocial interventions for mental and substance use disorders: A framework for establishing evidence-based standards*. Washington, DC: National Academies Press.

McHugh, R. K., & Barlow, D. H. (2010). Dissemination and implementation of evidence-based psychological interventions: A review of current efforts. *American Psychologist*, 65(2), 73–84.

Rauch, S. A. M., Yasinski, C. W., Post, L. M., Jovanovic, T. J., Norrholm, S. N., Sherrill, A. M., . . . Rothbaum, B. O. (In Press). An intensive outpatient program with prolonged exposure for veterans with posttraumatic stress disorder: Retention, predictors, and patterns of change. *Psychological Services*.

Contents

Acknowledgments

The authors would like to thank Ms. Megan Goodlin, Ms. Elizabeth Carbone, Ms. Danielle Wray, and Ms. Giselle Remy-Bryan for their consultation and assistance with the case management forms included in this manual. The authors would also like to thank Dr. Brittany Lannert, Dr. Michael Messina, and Dr. Katherine Porter for their consultation and assistance with the group in vivo exposure handouts on graded exposure.

CHAPTER 1

Foundations of Prolonged Exposure

Prolonged Exposure for Intensive Outpatient Programs (PE-IOP) outlines an adaptation of prolonged exposure (PE) therapy for use in a 2-week intensive outpatient program (IOP) mental health setting. It includes a therapist guide as well as patient handouts (see Appendix A). This combined individual and group treatment protocol incorporates the key components of PE therapy that were developed to ameliorate the symptoms of posttraumatic stress disorder (PTSD). This guide is intended to be an addendum to the PE guide for individual psychotherapy (Foa, Hembree, Rothbaum, & Rauch, 2019). Thus, it provides guidance for the adaptation of individual PE to a combined individual and group format in an IOP setting while retaining the key components of individual PE. Such models, where sessions are provided on a daily basis, are often referred to as "massed." This guide is written for mental health providers, such as psychologists, social workers, and psychiatric nurses, who have been trained in the implementation of individual PE. Providers who utilize this protocol should be trained in the implementation of individual PE. Mental health providers who have not received specialty training in PE should first obtain training in individual PE and only then utilize this therapist guide.

Background Information and Purpose of Emotional Processing

The overall aim of the treatment is to help trauma survivors *emotionally process* their traumatic experiences to diminish or eliminate PTSD and other trauma-related symptoms. The term "prolonged exposure" reflects the fact that the treatment program emerged from the long tradition of exposure therapy for anxiety disorders in which patients are helped to confront safe but anxiety-evoking situations to overcome their unrealistic, excessive fear and anxiety. At the same time, PE has emerged from the extension of emotional processing theory (EPT) to PTSD, which emphasizes the central role of successfully processing the traumatic memory in the amelioration of PTSD symptoms. Throughout this guide, we highlight that emotional processing is the mechanism underlying successful reduction of PTSD symptoms.

PE includes the following key components:

- *Education* about common reactions to trauma, what maintains trauma-related symptoms, and how PE reduces PTSD symptoms.
- Repeated *in vivo* confrontation with situations, people, or objects that the patient is avoiding because they are reminders of the trauma and cause emotional distress, such as anxiety, shame, or guilt.
- Repeated *imaginal exposure* to the trauma memories (i.e., revisiting and recounting the trauma memory in imagery) followed by processing the details of the event, the emotions, and the thoughts that the patient experienced during the trauma. This is accomplished through discussion of the experience of recounting the trauma memories.

The aim of in vivo and imaginal exposure is to enhance emotional processing of traumatic events by helping the patient face the trauma memories and reminders and process the emotions and thoughts as well as the details of the trauma that emerge during the revisiting experiences. In doing so, *patients learn that talking and thinking about the trauma are not the same as being in the trauma.* They learn that

- they can safely experience these trauma reminders,
- the distress that initially results from confrontations with these reminders decreases over time, and
- they can tolerate this distress.

They also learn to examine their negative emotions and thoughts about themselves (such as anxiety, shame, and guilt) and their emotions and thoughts about the world as an entirely dangerous place and determine if they are unrealistic and thus should be abandoned or modified. Ultimately, the treatment helps patients reclaim their lives from the devastating consequences of PTSD symptoms.

Prolonged exposure has been developed over the past 30 years through well-controlled studies and clinical practice in which PE was provided to thousands of patients. In addition, thousands of therapists in a variety of settings and countries have been trained to implement the treatment. Our clinical experiences and the results of numerous studies over the years have guided the evolution of PE to being delivered in this 2-week intensive outpatient format, which is detailed in the chapters that follow. The model can be extended to 3 weeks for patients who are responding but not yet remitted.

PE has become one of the most studied psychotherapeutic interventions, with hundreds of completed efficacy and effectiveness trials using gold standard randomized clinical trial methodologies. Studies have compared PE's impact with other treatments including medications, cognitive processing therapy (CPT), eye movement desensitization and reprocessing (EMDR), and counseling and have examined the value of adding other techniques such as cognitive restructuring, relaxation, and stress inoculation training (SIT). In general, adding other treatments for PTSD to PE did not improve the outcome of PE alone and added to the demands on the patient and the therapist.

PE is a highly effective, flexible, and robust treatment for PTSD that can be safely and effectively applied with even the most complex patient presentations and comorbidities. Across the research to date, several meta-analyses of PE have indicated that PE is highly effective at ameliorating the symptoms of PTSD, depression, anxiety, guilt, suicidal ideation, and self-injurious behavior, and, in comparison with other forms of cognitive behavioral therapy (CBT), it achieved comparable outcomes (Cusack et al., 2016; Lee et al., 2016; Watts et al., 2013).

PE Treatment Mechanisms Research

Numerous studies have been conducted to better understand how treatments such as PE work, with the aim of further refining and improving the efficacy and efficiency of the treatment and of better understanding the psychopathology of anxiety disorders. These will be briefly summarized.

EPT posits two necessary conditions for emotional processing: (1) the fear structure must be activated to modify it, and (2) new information must be incorporated into the fear structure. This new information is encoded during exposure, altering the fear structure and leading to a general pattern of reduction in negative affect (habituation/extinction) as the same or similar stimuli are encountered, thereby resulting in symptom reduction. Thus, three potential indicators of emotional processing include (1) activation of the fear, (2) within-session extinction, and (3) between-session extinction. Accordingly, from EPT we hypothesize that the degree of fear activation (emotional engagement), the degree of fear reduction within sessions, and reduction of peak responses in successive exposure sessions will all be positively associated with improvement in PTSD symptom severity. Negative cognitions were hypothesized to impede recovery after a traumatic experience, and reduction of these cognitions is viewed as a key mechanism of emotional processing and the resultant recovery (Foa & Cahill, 2001; Foa & Rauch, 2004; Zalta et al., 2014).

Negative Trauma-Related Cognitions

The unhelpful, negative cognitions that "the world is extremely dangerous" and "I am extremely weak and incompetent" mediate the development and maintenance of PTSD by promoting avoidance that prevents disconfirmation. Accordingly, treatment that aims to ameliorate PTSD symptoms should change these erroneous cognitions by introducing new information that disconfirms these erroneous, negative cognitions (Foa, Huppert, & Cahill, 2006). Several lines of research support the hypothesis that reductions in negative trauma-related cognitions are a key mechanism of recovery from PTSD (e.g., Foa & Rauch, 2004; Kleim et al., 2013; Moser, Hajcak, Simons, & Foa, 2007; Rauch et al., 2015; Zalta et al., 2014). Providing strongest support for change in cognitions as a possible causative mechanism, research examining the temporal sequencing of change has shown that reductions in negative trauma-related cognitions temporally precede decreases in PTSD symptoms during PE (Kumpula et al., 2017; Foa & McLean, 2016; McLean, Su, & Foa, 2014; McLean, Yeh, Rosenfield, & Foa, 2015; Zalta et al., 2014), whereas PTSD symptom reduction did not precede reduction in negative cognitions. These findings are consistent with the EPT supposition that change in negative cognitions is involved in PTSD recovery, whether it be natural recovery or therapeutic recovery, whether it is due to PE or to another PTSD treatment (Foa et al., 2006).

Fear Activation (Emotional Engagement)

The role of emotional engagement in PTSD treatment has been examined by Foa and colleagues using several methods. One study that operationalized emotional engagement as facial fear expression during the first session of imaginal exposure found that higher fear expression was associated with superior treatment outcome after PE (Foa, Riggs, Massie, & Yarczower, 1995). Research findings from extinction learning paradigms (often conceptualized as an analogue to exposure therapy) in animals lend support to the hypothesis that greater fear activation during exposure therapy is associated with greater reductions in PTSD symptoms. Benzodiazepine medications reduce arousal and are not recommended for patients with PTSD, especially those in treatment. Indeed, in one study they were found to impede response to exposure therapy in veterans with PTSD (Rothbaum et al., 2014).

Within- and Between-Session Extinction (Habituation)

As noted earlier, EPT originally proposed that the gradual reduction of anxiety within a session is an indicator of emotional processing, which is the process by which pathological anxiety is reduced. Although anxiety does typically decline from the beginning to the end of an exposure session, the role of within-session extinction in treatment outcomes has not received strong support (Jaycox, Foa, & Morral, 1998; Nacasch et al., 2015; van Minnen & Hagenaars, 2002; see Craske et al., 2008, for a review). Indeed, since PE was first developed, a robust literature related to extinction learning in animals and humans has indicated that within-session fear reduction is not related to fear extinction (i.e., long-term fear reduction). These findings have clinical implications because they suggest that shortening exposure sessions may be feasible without reducing treatment efficacy. Indeed, although longer exposures have been shown to promote greater within-session extinction than shorter exposures (e.g., van Minnen & Foa, 2006), the fact that within-session fear reduction does not predict treatment outcome suggests that the length of PE sessions can be shortened if necessary without compromising efficacy.

In contrast to within-session extinction, between-session extinction has been associated with therapeutic recovery in many studies (e.g., Rauch et al., 2004; Sripada & Rauch, 2015; van Minnen & Foa, 2006; Nacasch et al., 2015) but not all (e.g., Pitman et al., 1996). Consequently, EPT has shifted away from a focus on within-session extinction toward a model emphasizing emotional engagement, disconfirmation (i.e., change in negative cognitions), and between-session extinction.

Benefits and Risks of This Treatment Program

Benefits

Thirty years of research on PE, as partially summarized earlier, has yielded findings that clearly support the robust and versatile efficacy of PE as a treatment for PTSD resulting from a wide range of traumatic experiences and when delivered to complex patients. Nearly all studies have found that PE reduces not only PTSD but also other trauma-related problems, including depression, general anxiety, anger, self-injurious behaviors, and guilt. PE provides an avenue for transformative change in helping people to reclaim their lives from PTSD.

Risks

The primary risks associated with PE therapy are temporary discomfort and emotional distress when confronting anxiety-provoking images, memories, and situations in the course of treatment. The procedures of PE are intended to promote engagement with the range of emotions associated with the traumatic memory (e.g., anxiety, fear, sadness, anger, shame, guilt) to help the patient process the traumatic memories. During PE the therapist not only should be supportive and empathic in guiding the patient through the processing of the trauma memory but also should monitor the patient's distress and intervene when necessary to modulate the level of emotional engagement and associated discomfort. When recommending PE to a trauma survivor, the therapist should explain that disclosing trauma-related information and working to emotionally process these painful experiences in therapy may initially lead to increased emotional distress and, for some people, a temporary exacerbation of PTSD, anxiety, and depression. This is described to patients as "feeling worse before you feel better." However, in a sample of 75 women receiving PE for assault-related PTSD, this temporary exacerbation occurred in a small subset of patients and was not associated with worse outcome or with premature termination of treatment (Foa, Zoellner, Feeny, Hembree, & Alvarez-Conrad, 2002). Moreover, while some patients fail to benefit from this therapy, there are only a handful of case reports of symptoms worsening after exposure therapy. In fact, recent studies have shown that individuals who drop out of PE before completion do not show significant increases in severity of PTSD and depression (Tuerk et al., 2011).

Alternative Treatments

Although an extensive review of studies investigating CBT treatments for PTSD is beyond the scope of this therapist guide, our own research findings are neither unique nor isolated. In general, many studies over the past 30 years have found exposure therapy effective in reducing PTSD and other trauma-related pathology, rendering it the most empirically validated approach among the psychosocial treatments for PTSD and one designated by expert treatment guidelines as a first-line treatment (American Psychological Association [APA], 2017, Foa, Keane, Friedman, & Cohen, 2009; Institute of Medicine [IOM], 2007; VA/DOD, 2017). In addition to PE and other variants of exposure therapy, the CBT programs that have been empirically examined and found effective include CPT, SIT, cognitive therapy (CT), and EMDR. For a recent meta-analyses comparing interventions, see Lee et al. (2016) and Watts et al. (2013).

The Role of Medications

The VA/DOD and American Psychological Association's 2017 PTSD practice guidelines recommend the selective serotonergic reuptake inhibitors (SSRIs) sertraline (Zoloft), paroxetine (Paxil), and fluoxetine

(Prozac) and the serotonin norepinephrine reuptake inhibitor (SNRI) venlafaxine (Effexor) as pharmacological treatments for PTSD (APA, 2017; VA/DOD, 2017). Of these, the only medications with US Food and Drug Administration support as a treatment of PTSD are two SSRIs: sertraline and paroxetine. A number of randomized controlled trials have found SSRIs to be superior to placebo, and most studies of SSRIs have generally found a significant reduction in all symptom clusters of PTSD. They are also considered useful agents because of their efficacy in improving comorbid disorders such as depression, panic disorder, and obsessive-compulsive disorder and because of their relatively low side-effect profile.

There has been interest in combining more novel medications with psychotherapy, particularly for patients who are considered treatment resistant. These medications include d-cycloserine (Mataix-Cols et al., 2017; Rothbaum et al., 2014), 3,4-methylenedioxymethamphetamine (MDMA) (Mithoefer, Wagner, Mithoefer, Jerome, & Doblin, 2011), cannabinoids (Rabinak et al., 2014), and methylene blue (Zoellner et al., 2017). Note that these novel medications are not recommended by either treatment guideline (APA, 2017; VA/DOD, 2017).

Why We Created a Therapist Guide for Intensive Outpatient Prolonged Exposure

As providers of standard individual format PE for more than 30 years, we are driven by the excellent outcomes that PE can provide for patients who attend sessions and complete an adequate dose of care, and we are challenged by the difficulties that patients with PTSD have in attending *any* treatment course long enough to receive a therapeutic dose. Across PTSD interventions—whether focused on medications or different types of psychotherapy—in standard clinical care, retention rates are low, with about half of patients who start a course of care never actually receiving enough to consider the dose adequate. Using the model presented in this therapist guide to provide PE in an intensive outpatient model of care results in previously unseen retention rates for PTSD treatment, with more than 90% of patients typically completing the course of care.

Over the years of using PE-IOP, we have been convinced by our patient's outcomes, retention, and self-report that this model overcomes the avoidance that pervades PTSD. Specifically, patient after patient recounts previous episodes of PTSD treatment in weekly outpatient format where they would come and do their best in session only to have to pack it all in and return home to work and family at the end of the session. The next week they would drive back to session and open up, but each time it was a difficult choice. Indeed, many did not make that choice to go back for session 2 or 3 or 4. The PE-IOP model allows patients with PTSD to make the choice to approach instead of avoid *once*, when they come to Day 1. Once they are here, the whole milieu of the program is built to help them maintain that choice to continue to approach the memory and reminders until it no longer carries the emotional intensity and power that fuels PTSD.

In addition to addressing the issue of retention, PE-IOP can address both access and quality of provider training/fidelity. For programs that include housing patients for 2–3 weeks, use of a PE-IOP model allows for specific specialized centers of care that can be accessed by people from across the country or even from around the world to receive top-notch PTSD treatment from providers who are steeped in the treatment of PTSD and the provision of high-fidelity PE to obtain the best possible outcomes for diverse and complex patients. PE-IOP combats access problems by accommodating out-of-town referrals and improves PE quality through a tight-knit team and milieu all focused on PE.

This therapist guide for PE-IOP is designed for use by a therapist who is familiar with CBT and who has undergone an intensive training workshop for PE by experts in this therapy. While a chapter focuses on variations in the model, including length of the program, the primary model presented is 2 weeks in duration. The guide will instruct therapists to implement this brief CBT program that targets individuals who are diagnosed with PTSD or who manifest PTSD symptoms that cause distress and/or dysfunction following various types of trauma. This guide is intended for providers who already have standard PE training and programs based in PE who want to branch out into this specialized model for PTSD treatment, one intended to give those suffering with PTSD what they want in the format that fits PTSD rather than having patients fit into our standard mental health model of weekly care. Some of the material in the guide is taken from the standard PE guide (*Prolonged Exposure Therapy for PTSD: Emotional Processing of Traumatic Experiences Therapist Guide*, second edition [Foa, Hembree, Rothbaum, & Rauch, 2019]) and from the standard PE patient workbook (*Reclaiming Your Life from a Traumatic Experience Workbook*, second edition [Rothbaum, Foa, Hembree, & Rauch, 2019]) with only slight modifications for this setting. This is intentional, as we see this model as providing the same intervention components and rationale but with a variation in format.

CHAPTER 2

Posttraumatic Stress Disorder Treatment in Intensive Outpatient (IOP) Format

Need for a New Treatment Format

As noted at the end of Chapter 1, clinicians and researchers started examining models for more frequent or "massed" sessions in order to address two problems in the treatment of posttraumatic stress disorder (PTSD):

- The first problem is that less than 50% of patients who start an episode of PTSD treatment (medication or psychotherapy) will complete the standard treatment. The mental health system is set up for the standard model of weekly or even less than weekly contact with a provider during treatment. Since PTSD is a disorder characterized by avoidance, treatment may require frequent sessions to motivate the patient to accomplish the exposure exercises. Instead, the frequency of the sessions is set up to accommodate the system rather than patient needs.

- The second problem is lack of access to providers with specialized training in utilizing effective PTSD-focused psychotherapy and medication management. While the Veterans' Administration (VA) and US Department of Defense (DOD) have tried to increase access to specialized PTSD providers through dissemination of training programs, access remains limited even in these systems. For patients outside of these systems of care, finding a provider trained in prolonged exposure (PE), cognitive processing therapy, eye movement desensitization and reprocessing (EMDR), or effective medication management for PTSD is extremely difficult, even in metropolitan areas. Finding trained providers in remote or rural areas is nearly impossible. Insurance coverage and financial constraints further limit this access for civilian patients.

Blount and colleagues (Blount, Cigrang, Foa, Ford, & Peterson, 2014) presented a case study of the first published model using PE in a massed format. They used a 2-week, 10-session model of daily PE where—using the PE manual (Foa, Hembree, & Rothbaum, 2007)—in vivo exposure started on Day 2 and imaginal exposure started on Day 3. The patient showed remission of PTSD and depressive symptoms that was maintained to 6-month follow-up, thus demonstrating that this model of care is acceptable, feasible, and effective. Encouraged by the possibility of this model of care, many clinical research groups began putting together intensive outpatient (IOP) formats with PE.

These published IOP-PE models have varied in length, but most range from 8 days (Van Woudenberg et al., 2018) to 4 weeks (Beidel, Frueh et al., 2017; Beidel, Stout et al., 2017; Oprel et al., 2018). Outcomes have been excellent across these models, with both civilian and military traumas and significant comorbidities showing large effect size reductions in both PTSD and depression. For those studies that examined follow-up, the gains have been maintained. Specifically, Van Woudenberg and colleagues developed a massed PE combined with EMDR format provided over 8 days, where patients received PE in the morning and EMDR in the afternoon, with physical exercise in between. Patients had all experienced multiple traumas and mixed trauma types. Both interventions were provided individually, with physical activities and psychoeducation provided in a group format. PTSD symptoms were reduced, with large effects sizes (Cohen's d's of 1.3 or higher) in this complex, comorbid, and multiply traumatized sample. Of note, a majority maintained those gains through 6-month follow-up (Van Woudenberg et al., 2018). In a separate analysis looking at the response of those patients with the dissociative subtype of PTSD, results showed that dissociative patients demonstrated PTSD and depressive symptom reductions that were not significantly different from non-dissociative patients (Zoet, 2018).

Beidel and colleagues (Beidel, Stout et al., 2017) have developed a mixed model of PTSD treatment combining exposure therapy, groups, and social and emotional rehabilitation with several varied specific programs ranging from 3 to 17 weeks (Beidel, Frueh et al., 2017; Beidel, Stout et al., 2017; Beidel et al., 2019). A controlled pilot of a 3-week protocol showed large reductions in PTSD and depression maintained to 6-month follow-up (Beidel, Frueh et al., 2017). In a randomized controlled trial (RCT) comparing trauma management therapy (TMT) plus virtual reality exposure therapy (VRE) to VRE alone, provided over 17 weeks (massed exposure over 5 weeks), significant and large reductions in PTSD and depression were shown in both conditions with no difference between conditions (Beidel et al., 2019). In addition, the changes were maintained to 6-month follow-up (Beidel et al., 2019). The group that received the additional TMT-focused group modules showed additional increases specifically in social interaction that was directly targeted in the TMT group.

In the first RCT comparing massed PE (10 sessions over 2 weeks) to spaced PE (10 sessions over 8 weeks), there was no difference in outcomes across the two PE conditions, but massed PE showed a 13.6% rate of drop while spaced showed a 24.8% drop during the treatment phase (Foa et al., 2018).

In an examination of longer term outcomes of IOP treatment for PTSD in Australia, using a model focused on exposure therapy though not specifically PE, Humphreys, Westerink, Giarratano, and Brooks (1999) reported maintenance of gains in military-related PTSD patients to 2 years posttreatment. This model provided a 4-week inpatient phase followed by at least 6 months of individual and group follow-up.

Of note, Hendriks and colleagues have also effectively used a massed PE model with adolescents with comorbid PTSD presentations including comorbidity and multiple trauma exposures (Hendriks et al., 2017). In this protocol, adolescents received three sessions of PE per day for 5 days followed by 3 weekly booster PE sessions. In this pilot study, 80% reached remission with this course of care, with no dropout or adverse events (Hendriks et al., 2017).

In 2015, with substantial support from the Wounded Warrior Project, four academic medical centers across the country—Emory University in the South, Massachusetts General Hospital in the Northeast, Rush University Medical Center in the Midwest, and the University of California, Los Angeles, in the West—established the Warrior Care

Network. As part of this initiative, we have expanded outpatient services for post–September 11 veterans and their families and developed innovative IOP programs to provide service personnel from across the country with care for PTSD, related mental health conditions, and traumatic brain injury (TBI). To date, our network has treated more than a thousand individuals, and the requests for services from veterans and their families continue to escalate (Pollack, Simon, & Rothbaum, 2017). Of note, Harvey and colleagues (2017) reported that 95% of veterans who entered the IOP programs completed the program. Two of the four sites focused their new IOP programs for PTSD around PE. Harvey and colleagues (2018) reported on their 2-week PTSD IOP designed around a core of PE for PTSD and supportive services for wellness and comorbid issues; this program showed large reductions in PTSD, depression, and self-reported TBI symptoms. Yasinski et al. (2018) and Rauch et al. (in press) reported preliminary outcomes from the Emory Healthcare Veterans Program's 2-week PTSD-focused IOP that is built on a core of daily PE with imaginal exposure starting at Day 2 and continuing through the end of the second week. In addition to PE, patients receive wellness and positive coping components (see Chapter 6 in this therapist guide) that focus on increasing the ability to maintain gains over time and find new value and life goals at the same time as reducing PTSD and related issues with PE. Of note, more than 90% of patients complete the 2-week program and show large effect size reductions in PTSD, depression, and self-reported TBI symptoms, with maintenance of gains out to 1 year (Rauch, Yasinski et al., in press).

Based on this growing body of literature supporting massed models of exposure therapy for PTSD, we have developed the current therapist guide for PE-IOP to reflect what appears to be the most effective model of care. Throughout the guide, we will present the model representing the most efficient and effective use of the principles of PE based in Emotional Processing Theory, extinction learning, and the best of what we know about effective PTSD care. We will specify those pieces that should not be varied or only varied with caution and an examination of their impact on treatment response, as well as those areas where variation would be less likely to impact patient response.

CHAPTER 3

IOP Assessment and Structure

For Whom is PE-IOP Appropriate?

Any well-designed treatment program begins with assessment. Just like standard prolonged exposure (PE), the Prolonged Exposure-Intensive Outpatient Program (PE-IOP) is a treatment for posttraumatic stress disorder (PTSD) or moderate to severe PTSD symptoms that cause distress or decrease functioning. PTSD is most often accompanied by other mental health issues. The PE-IOP model is well-suited to treat PTSD alone and in the context of complex and significant comorbidities and trauma histories. As a plus, PE-IOP demonstrates very high rates of retention, especially when compared to standard weekly outpatient models of care. Indeed, PE-IOP patients report that this model worked for them because they did not have to make the choice to attend sessions every week but just once at the beginning of care. IOP is a model well-suited for this avoidance-based disorder.

Standard PE has been studied across thousands of patients and has strong support for its use. While the format of PE-IOP is different, the intervention remains essentially the same, and early research effects using PE-IOP are at least as good as standard PE with much higher retention. Typically, more than 90% of patients who start PE-IOP complete treatment (Foa et al., 2018; Yasinski et al., 2018; Rauch et al., in press). On the basis of treating and studying thousands of trauma survivors with PE and recent studies and clinical program outcomes with PE-IOP, we recommend that PE-IOP be considered for use with:

- *Individuals with PTSD or distressing PTSD symptoms and related psychopathology (e.g., depression, chronic anxiety, anger or shame, axis II disorders) following all types of trauma.* If full diagnostic criteria are not met, the patient should still have significant symptoms of the disorder that are distressing and interfering.
- *Individuals with sufficient memory of the traumatic event(s) that they have a narrative*: they can describe the trauma memory (verbally or in writing), and the story has a beginning, middle, and end. Gaps can occur, but there needs to be some memory to follow.

The presence of any of the following comorbid difficulties should take priority in clinical intervention, and PE-IOP should not be implemented until after such intervention has occurred and the condition is stabilized:

- *Imminent threat of suicidal or homicidal behavior.* While current suicidal ideation and even history of suicide gestures or attempts are quite common in our PTSD patients, if the person is currently at high risk for acting on these impulses, the suicidal or homicidal behavior requires clinical attention and stabilization prior to initiation of trauma-focused treatment.
- *Serious self-injurious behavior.* It is not unusual for PTSD patients to present with histories of cutting, burning, or otherwise deliberately injuring themselves. If that type of self-injurious behavior is currently active, PE-IOP should be deferred until the person has acquired skills or tools to manage these impulses without acting on them. In our studies, we typically require a period of at least 3 months with no serious self-injurious behavior and a commitment by the patients to use his tools to manage self-harming impulses that may arise. During treatment, we tell patients that they may have urges to harm themselves but that it is not an option during treatment with PE because they need to learn that they can tolerate their negative emotions and that those emotions will decrease without efforts to escape, avoid, or distract.
- *Current psychosis.* After years of refraining from using PE with individuals with psychotic disorder diagnoses, we have begun to offer treatment to patients with such history *if they are stabilized on appropriate medications and currently not exhibiting psychotic symptoms.*

We have had success with these individuals, but PE has not been systematically studied with this population. The residential setting that allows for more patient contact may be especially helpful with such complex presentations if the team is aware of the comorbidity and is able to work together to address it as needed.

- *Current high risk of being assaulted (e.g., living with domestic violence).* Many of our patients have lived in dangerous environments that carry a significant risk of negative events and were successfully treated with PE. But if your patient is currently in a living situation in which he is being beaten, sexually assaulted, or seriously harmed, ensuring safety or removal from the dangerous situation should be the focus of intervention. Safety is paramount. PE-IOP should be delayed until the person is away from this ongoing violent living situation and the symptoms have had time to stabilize.

In addition to these exclusionary criteria, there are several other commonly encountered issues you may need to consider specific to the IOP context in determining whether to offer a trauma survivor treatment with PE-IOP.

- *Alcohol and substance use should be assessed.* For most patients able to commit to 2 weeks without using substances, PE-IOP can be an excellent fit. Based on assessment and patient willingness to include alcohol or substance use goals in their treatment plan, the treatment team may consider several options for inclusion in the treatment plan, including (1) psychoeducation about the interplay of alcohol and substance use and PTSD, (2) simultaneous alcohol or substance use disorder (SUD)-based cognitive-behavioral therapy (CBT) intervention such as COPE, and/or (3) monitoring of use and periodic breathalyzer/urine drug screens as needed throughout the PE-IOP. Significant levels of alcohol and other substances may interfere with learning pace and progress. If the patient is unable to commit to 2 weeks without using during the program, or if use is such that the treatment team is concerned for the safety of the patient or his ability to learn and profit from treatment, then preparatory use of an alcohol or SUD-based intervention may be warranted and would certainly include a medical or specialized SUD assessment. Within the area of PTSD, medical and nonmedical marijuana use is a significant issue of note. As with any substance, use should be assessed and discussed with the patient. Attention to marijuana laws across state lines (for patients coming to a program) should be considered and discussed as well. Finally, given the lack of specific research to support the use of marijuana in PTSD treatment, providers should suggest to patients that it is best to abstain for the duration of the program; clinicians at the very least should ask patients not to use prior to exposures, before any treatment component, or to cope with distress.

- *Current medical issues that would interfere with engaging in PTSD treatment also need to be assessed.* Most patients with chronic PTSD have additional mental and physical health issues, such as severe depression, migraines, high blood pressure, or chronic pain. In-depth assessment of past and current medications and medical issues is warranted to ensure that while patients are in the PE-IOP they will be able to fully focus on PTSD. In addition, we do not want patients to put their physical health at risk by engaging in exercise if they have an injury or unmanaged high blood pressure, etc.

Living or Working in a High-Risk Environment

It is reasonable to question whether PE-IOP will be effective for someone who lives in a dangerous area or has a hazardous job that carries a significant risk of harm. Examples of this abound: the person living in a war-torn country, the woman living in a violent neighborhood, and the active-duty marine who will soon be deployed overseas for another tour of duty in a dangerous land. Can PE-IOP help someone whose life circumstances increase the likelihood of being exposed to a trauma after their PE-IOP treatment? Our experiences in both the United States and abroad have taught us that the answer to this question is yes. If it has been determined that the person meets criteria for PTSD or has moderate to severe PTSD symptoms, then a significant part of the distress and avoidance he is experiencing is due to the traumas that happened in the past. While his symptoms may also be fueled by the realistic present-day risk of harm, they are increased due to the PTSD that resulted from previous exposure—amplifying his fear and expectations of harm in day-to-day life. When discussing the possibility of PE-IOP with a patient, the therapist can discuss:

I know that you have a hazardous job (or live in a hazardous place) and that this requires you to be vigilant. I also know that you have PTSD because of things that happened in the past, and this disorder causes people to exaggerate estimates of danger in their present life. What I suggest is that you and I work on helping you emotionally process the past trauma so that your PTSD symptoms will diminish, and then we will see what remains. We will do our best to plan your in vivo exposure exercises so that they will be useful to your recovery but will not carry a high risk of harm or danger. I think that when the PTSD symptoms related to your past trauma are reduced, you and I will be better able to address how you can live your life more comfortably given the day-to-day stresses you face. PTSD interferes with your ability to objectively judge the threat of some situations, so we hope when you complete this program, you will be able to judge the threat level more accurately.

This way of thinking about the situation often makes sense and is acceptable to patients with PTSD.

Military Service Members and Veterans

High risk of exposure to potentially traumatic events is often a part of military service. Estimates suggest that about 20% of those US service members deployed to the conflicts in Iraq and Afghanistan will suffer with PTSD in their lifetime (Hoge, Auchterlonie, & Milliken, 2006). PE has been used with military service members and veterans since its inception, and in the past 20 years we have seen an explosion of research with PE in these populations. Such research has supported the acceptability, safety, and effectiveness of PE in these populations, including in massed PE-IOP (Foa et al., 2018). Indeed, the most recent Veterans Administration/Department of Defense (VA/DOD) clinical practice guideline (VA/DOD, 2017) suggests the use of trauma-focused therapies (such as PE) first in their treatment algorithm, prior to medication.

Traumatic Brain Injury

Especially among military populations, traumatic brain injury (TBI) and PTSD often co-occur. Rates of comorbidity in veterans seeking treatment for PTSD suggest that about 22% also report probable TBI (Sripada et al., 2013). Conversely, about 34% of those Iraq and Afghanistan veterans who experienced a TBI also had probable PTSD (Tanielian et al., 2008). Of importance, effectiveness studies among patients with both PTSD and mild to moderate TBI support the acceptability, safety, and effectiveness of PE in addressing PTSD severity with minimal to no modifications to protocol (Ragsdale, Neer, Beidel, Frueh, & Stout, 2013; Ragsdale et al., 2019; Ragsdale & Voss Horrell, 2016; Sripada et al., 2013; Wolf et al., 2015).

Severe Dissociative Symptoms

Clinicians sometimes express reservations about using exposure therapy to treat patients with severe dissociative symptoms due to concern that the exposure will increase their dissociation. We do not routinely exclude these individuals from our PTSD treatment studies and neither have investigators of other large-scale clinical trials. In fact, recent studies examining whether dissociation is associated with poor outcome in PE therapy have found no evidence of this, even with severe or high levels of such symptoms. For example, Hagenaars, Van Minnen, and Hoogduin (2010) report that dissociative symptoms including emotional numbing, depersonalization, and general tendency to dissociate were not predictive of poor treatment outcome or premature dropout among 70 patients receiving PE. Moreover, patients reporting high levels of numbing had better outcomes than patients with lower levels of numbing. We agree with van Minnen, Harned, Zoellner, and Mills (2012) that dissociation is in effect a form of avoidance that contributes to the maintenance of PTSD symptoms by impeding emotional processing. In this regard PE is a most fitting treatment as it encourages patients to reduce avoidance behavior in the service of healing PTSD.

However, if a patient's dissociative symptoms so outweigh PTSD-related symptoms in severity and in degree of interference that it is not possible to implement PE effectively, the patient may not be able to benefit from the treatment. In such cases, as when other disorders are of primary clinical importance (i.e., severe depression with high suicidal risk, severe drug dependence), the more severe disorder should take precedence in clinical intervention, and PE should be implemented afterward. Thus, in considering whether to use PE with such patients, we recommend that you consider the severity of the dissociative symptoms relative to the PTSD. Clinicians and patients should discuss the factors that contribute to dissociation and consider how to implement exposure exercises in a manner that minimizes dissociation. For example, the patient can learn to utilize grounding techniques when needed. Patients often experience this as a great success and mastery experience over symptoms that may feel frightening and out of control.

Presence of Personality Disorders

We do not exclude patients from PE on the basis of meeting criteria for personality disorder. In fact, it has been clearly established that many individuals with chronic PTSD do have comorbid personality disorders, and our treatment population is consistent with this finding. Two studies have been conducted comparing the outcomes of women with and without personality disorders who were treated for assault-related chronic PTSD. No significant differences in improvement in PTSD between those with and without personality disorder were found in either study (Feeny, Zoellner, & Foa, 2002; Hembree, Cahill, & Foa, 2004). Both studies showed that, compared to individuals without personality disorder diagnosis, those with personality disorders tended to have higher scores on psychopathology scales (e.g., severity of PTSD, depression) at both pre- and posttreatment assessment points, but the degree of improvement was the same for the two groups. van Minnen et al. (2012) also reported that personality traits were not predictive of either outcome or dropout from PE. In general, neither personality characteristics nor personality disorders have been found to predict poorer outcome with PE, and these individuals should be offered PE.

The majority of studies that have examined the impact of personality disorder on response to PE have been focused on individuals with borderline personality disorder (BPD) and PTSD. van Minnen et al. (2012) reviewed this literature and concluded that there is no empirical support for excluding patients with BPD from PE who meet the eligibility criteria specified in this PE-IOP therapist guide. However, some individuals with severe degrees of personality disorder may be excluded from PE-IOP because of safety reasons (e.g., an individual with BPD with a suicide plan and intent or current serious self-injurious or destructive behavior). These patients may do well with a combination of PE and dialectic behavioral therapy (DBT). Several studies of combined PE and DBT (Harned, Korslund, Foa, & Linehan, 2012; Harned, Korslund, & Linehan, 2014) have shown very promising results with patients who are typically excluded from PE outcome studies because of safety reasons.

PTSD Accompanied by Prominent Guilt or Shame

Individuals with PTSD sometimes experience prominent guilt or shame, such as the rape survivor who thinks he should have prevented the rape and blames himself for being where he was or for not fighting hard enough, or the soldier who killed someone in the line of duty. The term *moral injury* is sometimes used within military populations to describe experiences where a trauma survivor feels guilt, and his sense of right and wrong in the world has been shaken (see later discussion). Guilt and shame may also be prominent in cases where the patient harmed another person accidentally, or in a situation where the person committed a violent act in a moment of extreme stress or rage. In instances of *perceived perpetration*—where a survivor feels guilt for something he did or did not do at the time of a trauma—PE has shown to be very effective in reducing shame, guilt, and PTSD severity (Smith, Duax, & Rauch, 2013). For PTSD cases where guilt is a primary emotion, we recommend that ample time be devoted to addressing the guilt. Imaginal exposure to the trauma memory will help the patient view the trauma in context and, along with the following processing, will help him put the events in realistic perspective. Processing in such cases would include discussion of the context of the trauma and the meaning this holds about the self at the time of the trauma and now. These cases may include discussion of the context of the trauma that led to the choices made during it and the sharing of responsibility with others, which may include the patient, his command, his comrades on the mission, the insurgent, etc.

Anger

Anger is a core symptom of PTSD (American Psychiatric Association, 2013). Clinical lore has suggested that anger may interfere with psychotherapy outcomes, but empirical examinations have shown significant reductions in anger with PE and no difference in patient outcomes for those reporting higher versus lower levels of anger (Cahill, Rauch, Hembree, & Foa, 2004). Anger can be conceptualized as a form of avoidance of other more vulnerable emotions with which the trauma survivor may not want to engage. No specific intervention or modification of standard protocol is required for anger with PE unless the anger is so severe that it prevents approaching the trauma memory and reminders or causes other noncompliance with the elements of PE treatment.

Complex PTSD

While complex PTSD did not receive recognition in the *Diagnostic and Statistical Manual of Mental Disorders* (DSM-5; American Psychiatric Association, 2013), it continues to garner attention in the field of PTSD treatment providers. The validity of this diagnosis is a concept of significant debate (Cloitre, Garvert, Brewin, Bryant, & Maercker, 2013; Resick et al., 2012). Indeed, after a clinical treatment survey and recommendations for complex PTSD were put forward by the International Society for Traumatic Stress Studies (ISTSS) (Cloitre et al., 2011), many PTSD treatment leaders responded with a review of the treatment literature to date that suggests that PE is effective for patients who present with the issues that may be labeled as complex PTSD (de Jongh et al., 2016). Indeed, thorough assessment, including a differential diagnosis of PTSD and common comorbidities, may provide a more specific and effective treatment plan, with PE providing effective treatment of PTSD and many related comorbidities. For those issues that remain, treatment to address these issues would be warranted.

Moral Injury or Perceived Perpetration

Another construct that has gained some attention recently is *moral injury*. As with complex PTSD, this construct has not been consistently defined across research, thus leading to inconsistencies. Moral injury refers to a characteristic of a traumatic experience that occurs when the survivor perceives that his actions (or inactions) at the time of the trauma are not consistent with his values, resulting in guilt and shame. Such moral injuries can occur with any type of trauma; proponents of moral injury suggest that it is most often associated with combat trauma, although there is no study to support this view. Also, as noted earlier, a related construct relevant to PTSD treatment is *perceived perpetration*, which occurs when (a) a trauma survivor acted with potentially violent or lethal force or failed to act when violence was occurring to others, (b) interprets his behavior as perpetration or as violating his moral code, and (c) acted as a consequence of the trauma context and not as a premeditated act or with instrumental intent to victimize (Smith et al., 2013). Of note, PE has demonstrated clinical effectiveness in addressing PTSD resulting from moral injury and perceived perpetration.

Phone or In-Person Screen

With programs that include housing patients for 2–3 weeks, as described here, a screen is the first step. Typically, to minimize patient burden and maximize program efficiency, such screening occurs via phone. For those programs that treat patients who may reside in other states, this becomes even more important to minimize the occurrence of unexpected issues once the patient is on-site (such as imminent suicidal or homicidal risk or substance use in the residential setting). While beyond the scope of this book, programs must consider laws and practices regarding telehealth and care provided across state lines to ensure they are compliant. This may include a partial assessment by phone and confirmation of diagnoses when the patient arrives on site. In addition to the noted high-impact exclusionary criteria, programs should consider phone screens to look for the most common issues that would prevent the patient from benefitting from the IOP. Phone screens will require different levels of sensitivity depending on the program and its ability to handle patients who have more acute difficulties after arrival. Such screens should be brief and include rule-outs for:

- *Imminent risk of harm* to self or others or recent hospitalization due to risk of harm to self or others (within the past 60–90 days),
- *Stable housing to return to* following the program,
- *Ability to commit to not using alcohol or substances* for the length of the program,
- *Unmanaged bipolar or psychotic disorder*, and
- *Medical issues* that would prevent a focus on PTSD.

In addition, phone screens should include a rule-in assessment for a history of a criterion A event with associated symptoms of PTSD and to track a relevant assessment of history of TBI and alcohol or substance use disorder.

Once the phone screen is passed, additional assessment is warranted to ensure program fit and plan for treatment. Assessment occurs prior to entry into PE-IOP to ensure the fit between a patient with presenting difficulties and program goals. Assessment continues with self-report measures for PTSD and depression every other day while in the PE-IOP program, using measures with a treatment-relevant time period (such as the 1-week version of the Posttraumatic Stress Diagnostic Scale [PDS5] or PTSD Checklist [PCL5]). These measures are used to monitor progress and refine the program as needed so that the individual patient can maximize his gains. We will summarize key points in assessment in this chapter and expand on issues specific to the IOP format.

Intake Assessment Strategies

Initial assessment for PE-IOP should:

- *Obtain a detailed trauma history and determine the index or target trauma* (i.e., the trauma that seems to be associated with the current symptoms and should be the primary focus in treatment).
- *Confirm the diagnosis of PTSD* (or presence of significant symptoms) and determine its severity.
- *Assess for the presence of comorbid disorders.*
- *Review medical records* and previous treatment history and current physical and mental health treatments (including medications, etc.).
- *Establish the severity of any other current disorders* and whether they will require immediate intervention.

- *Ensure no contraindications for group PE-IOP components* (presence of severe personality issues that prevent successful group participation or previous history of violent acting-out or interfering with group progress).

The initial evaluation is conducted with the aid of both interviewer and self-report instruments. After review of medical records, we gather information regarding the history of Criterion A traumatic events and ascertain which is currently the most distressing and frequently reexperienced. To diagnose and assess the severity of PTSD, we use the Clinician Administered PTSD Scale-5 (Weathers et al., 2018) or the Posttraumatic Symptom Scale–Interview 5 (PSS-I5) measure (Foa, McLean et al., 2016). The Diagnostic Interview for Anxiety, Mood, and OCD and Related Neuropsychiatric Disorders (DIAMOND; Tolin et al., 2018) or the Structured Clinical Interview for DSM5 (First, Williams, Karg, & Spitzer, 2015) or other clinical interview is used to assess for the presence of comorbid disorders. Self-report measures may include the PDS5 (Foa, McLean et al., 2016) or the PCL5 (Blevins et al., 2015) and the Patient Health Questionnaire (PHQ-9) (Kroenke et al., 2001). Interview, medical records review, and self-report measures are used to confirm diagnosis and establish treatment plans. We obtain a release of information (ROI) and often talk to previous providers to clarify diagnostic issues, treatment goals, previous treatment, and opinions regarding propensity for violence or to act out with providers, patients, or in groups. Proactive planning for issues that may arise and how they may assist or impede treatment progress is critical. In addition, as you will see later, treatment plans are individualized to fit the specific presentation of the patient and his treatment goals. In addition to intake, self-report measures of PTSD and depression are used at program arrival and during treatment to monitor change and consider modifications to treatment plans when patients are progressing more quickly or slowly.

Goals of PE-IOP

The goals of PE-IOP are to

1. Reduce emotional reactivity related to the target trauma memory and increase function.
2. Provide information about the role of avoidance in the maintenance of PTSD symptoms.

3. Discourage use of negative coping and avoidance of trauma triggers, isolation, or safety behaviors that function to maintain anxiety and distress.

4. Challenge unhelpful cognitions surrounding beliefs of certain activities being unsafe when most others would consider them safe and the perception of oneself as weak, incompetent, and unable to cope with negative affect.

5. Encourage use of positive coping (i.e., social supports, exercise, relaxation, self-care, communication).

6. Provide support for patients to increase their sense of self-confidence and management of their symptoms.

PE-IOP Model Overview

This IOP is designed to deliver PE treatment daily (weekdays) for 2 weeks with a core of PE provided through daily individual imaginal exposure and processing treatment sessions (90 minutes) and daily group in vivo exposure therapy sessions (120 minutes). Patients in a 2-week PE-IOP should receive nine group in vivo sessions (the tenth is planned for on-own exposure practice) and nine imaginal exposure sessions. Alternate program models that have shown success have varied individual session duration (60 vs. 90 minutes) and frequency (twice vs. once per day). Alternative schedules will be discussed in Chapter 8. However, the core of the program remains PE with all three components (imaginal and processing, in vivo, and psychoeducation). Psychoeducation is provided through group in vivo sessions, with additional repetition in individual sessions. Imaginal exposure and processing is provided in individual sessions with homework repetition at least twice per day, outside of session. In vivo exposure is provided in group exposure sessions, with repeated practices occurring outside of session during the IOP day. We will focus on the model used in the Emory Healthcare Veterans Program (EHVP) but recognize that programs may vary in detail while maintaining the core of PE. Chapter 4 provides an in-depth description of how exposure is provided in PE-IOP. Table 4.1 (see pp. 50–51) covers a sample patient schedule showing how these pieces are all coordinated into a daily 2-week PE-IOP.

In addition to the core PTSD-focused intervention with PE, the PE-IOP model includes daily case management, medical assessment and management as needed, integrative wellness, and intervention for common comorbidities. These additional components are added to encourage patients to engage in new positive coping activities and progress toward new life goals as their PTSD symptoms are reduced. Of note, all integrative wellness and comorbid disorder interventions are clearly presented as such and are distinguished from the core interventions that directly address the symptoms of PTSD. In considering what interventions to add, ensure that the overall model and treatment rationale is consistent with the core intervention of PE.

Additional Programming

Case management provides:

1. Care coordination as patients come into and out of PE-IOP,
2. Logistic support for completion of the patient treatment work during IOP (i.e., transportation for in vivo exposures and arranging appointments for specific items needed for exposures), and
3. Aftercare planning focusing on next-step goals of how to maintain gains at home, increase social connection, and value consistent living.

Integrative wellness focuses on what the patient wants to do to increase his quality of life and community connection. Programs may vary in which integrative wellness components are included but should consider offering at least some of the following:

- nutrition,
- fitness or physical training,
- yoga,
- meditation,
- mindfulness,
- massage (for general stress management or pain), and/or
- acupuncture (for pain, sleep, or general stress management).

Patients set specific goals, with steps that can be started or completed during PE-IOP as well as working with case managers to maintain changes and take steps toward specific wellness goals at home. Our case managers are social workers, but programs can consider if other professions may fill this role.

Interventions for common comorbidities include some groups that are provided to all patients as well as groups that may be attended specifically based on the individual presentation. Specific groups may vary by program resources and provider expertise, but in EHVP, these include

- sleep,
- alcohol and SUD,
- pain,
- anger.

Readers are referred to Chapter 6 for more in-depth discussion of integrative wellness and interventions for comorbid issues.

How It All Fits

To get a real feel for how the pieces fit together, we provide an example daily schedule in Table 3.1. (Table 3.1 appears in this printed chapter in black and white; it is also available in color on the *Treatments ThatWork* Web site at www.oxfordclinicalpsych.com/PE-IOP.) These tables are intended to give an overview of the program, and the following chapters then go into the details of how the pieces are executed together.

Table 3.1 Emory Healthcare Veterans Program (EHVP) prolonged exposure-intensive outpatient (PE-IOP) patient schedule

Core Individual Imaginal Exposure
Core Group In Vivo Exposure
Case Management
Integrative Wellness
Medical Assessment and Management
Intervention for Comorbid Issues
Patient Practice
Other Activity or Break

Week 1: Day 1: Monday

Time	Activity	Provider(s)
6:30–7:15 AM	Breakfast	N/A
7:15–7:30 AM	Check-in	N/A
7:30–8:00 AM	Program Orientation	Patient Outreach Coordinators
8:00–8:30 AM	Case Management	Social Worker
8:30–10:00 AM	Additional Assessment as needed	Program Team
10:00–10:30 AM	Break	N/A
10:30–11:00 AM	Pre-Treatment Assessments	Program Team

11:00–1:00 PM	In Vivo-Group: Psychoeducation	Psychologist
1:00–1:30 PM	Lunch	N/A
2:00–3:00 PM	Labs	Program Team
3:00–4:00 PM	Substance Use Assessment	MD
4:00–4:30 PM	Break	N/A
4:30–5:30 PM	Acupuncture	Acupuncturist
5:30–6:00 PM	Break	N/A
6:00–7:30 PM	Nutritional Education over Dinner	MD or PhD

Week 1: Day 2: Tuesday

Time	Activity	Provider(s)
6:30–7:45 AM	Breakfast	N/A
7:45–8:00 AM	Check-in	N/A
8:00–8:30 AM	Case Management	Social Worker

8:30–9:30 AM	Break	N/A
9:30–11:00 AM	Individual Imaginal Exposure	Psychologist
11:00–1:00 PM	Group In Vivo Exposure	Psychologist
1:00–1:30 PM	Lunch	N/A
1:30–2:30 PM	Personal Training	Trainer
2:30–3:00 PM	Break	N/A
3:00–4:00 PM	IOP Medical Intake	Clinical Nurse or MD
4:00–4:30 PM	Break	N/A
4:30–5:30 PM	Sleep Education	Psychologist
5:30–6:30 PM	Wellness Program: Trauma Sensitive Yoga	Yoga Therapist
6:30–8:00 PM	Dinner	N/A

Week 1: Day 3: Wednesday

Time	Activity	Provider(s)
6:30–7:45 AM	Breakfast	N/A
7:45–8:00 AM	Check-in	N/A
8:00–8:30 AM	Case Management	Social Worker
8:30–9:00 AM	Treatment Surveys	Program Team
9:00–9:30 AM	Veteran Focused Case Management	VA Liaison
9:30–11:00 AM	Individual Imaginal Exposure	Psychologist
11:00–1:00 PM	Group In Vivo Exposure	Psychologist
1:00–2:00 PM	Wellness Meeting with Community Group	
2:00–3:00 PM	Break	N/A
3:00–4:00 PM	Medication Education Management	Clinical Nurse
4:00–5:30 PM	Acupuncture	Acupuncturist

Time	Activity	Provider(s)
5:30–6:30 PM	Wellness Program: Gentle Yoga	Yoga Therapist
6:30–8:00 PM	Dinner	N/A

Week 1: Day 4: Thursday

Time	Activity	Provider(s)
6:30–7:45 AM	Breakfast	N/A
7:45–8:00 AM	Check-in	N/A
8:00–8:30 AM	Case Management	Social Worker
8:30–9:30 AM	Wellness Session	Psychologist
9:30–11:00 AM	Individual Imaginal Exposure	Psychologist
11:00–1:00 PM	Group In Vivo Exposure	Psychologist
1:00–1:30 PM	Lunch	N/A
1:30–2:00 PM	Break	N/A

Time	Activity	Provider(s)
2:00–3:00 PM	Massage	Massage Therapist
3:00–3:30 PM	Break	N/A
3:30–4:30 PM	Finance and Careers	Patient Outreach Coordinator
4:30–5:30 PM	Relapse Prevention	Psychologist
5:30–6:30 PM	Wellness Program: Gentle Yoga	Yoga Therapist
6:30–8:00 PM	Dinner	N/A

Week 1: Day 5: Friday

Time	Activity	Provider(s)
6:30–7:45 AM	Breakfast	N/A
7:45–8:00 AM	Check-in	N/A
8:00–8:30 AM	Case Management	Social Worker
8:30–9:00 AM	Break	N/A
9:00–9:30 AM	Treatment Surveys	Program Team

9:30–11:00 AM	Individual Imaginal Exposure	Psychologist
11:00–12:30 PM	Group In Vivo Exposure	Psychologist
12:30–1:00 PM	Lunch	N/A
1:00–2:00 PM	Resource Workshop	Patient Outreach Coordinators
2:00–3:00 PM	Homework (if assigned)	On Own
3:00–4:30 PM	Family Focus: Individual Session	Psychologist
4:30–5:30 PM	Mindfulness Group	Psychologist
5:30–7:00 PM	Dinner	N/A

Weekend Activities:

- Practice in vivo exposures
- Listen to imaginal recording at least once per day
- Massage
- Outing (i.e., festival, sporting event, hike, etc.)

Week 2: Day 6: Monday

Time	Activity	Provider
6:30–7:45 AM	Breakfast	N/A
7:45–8:00 AM	Check-in	N/A
8:00–8:30 AM	Case Management	Social Worker
8:30–9:00 AM	Break	N/A
9:00–9:30 AM	Treatment Surveys	Program Team
9:30–11:00 AM	Individual Imaginal Exposure	Psychologist
11:00–1:00 PM	Group In Vivo Exposure	Psychologist
1:00 - 1:30 PM	Lunch	N/A
1:30–3:00 PM	Homework (if assigned)	On Own
3:00–4:00 PM	Acupuncture	Acupuncturist

Time	Activity	Provider(s)
4:00–6:00 PM	Break	N/A
6:00–7:30 PM	Nutritional Education over Dinner	MD or PhD

Week 2: Day 7: Tuesday

Time	Activity	Provider(s)
6:30–7:45 AM	Breakfast	N/A
7:45–8:00 AM	Check-in	N/A
8:00–8:30 AM	Case Management	Social Worker
8:30–9:30 AM	Break	N/A
9:30–11:00 AM	Individual Imaginal Exposure	Psychologist
11:00–1:00 PM	Group In Vivo Exposure	Psychologist
1:00–1:30 PM	Lunch	N/A

1:30–3:00 PM	Family Focus: Individual Session	Psychologist
3:00–4:30 PM	Homework (if assigned)	On Own
4:30–5:30 PM	Sleep Education	Psychologist
5:30–6:30 PM	Wellness Program: Gentle Yoga	Yoga Therapist
6:30–7:00 PM	Dinner	N/A
7:00–8:00 PM	Massage	Massage Therapist

Week 2: Day 8: Wednesday

Time	Activity	Provider(s)
6:30–7:45 AM	Breakfast	N/A
7:45–8:00 AM	Check-in	N/A
8:00–8:30 AM	Case Management	Social Worker
8:30–9:00 AM	Treatment Surveys	Research Team
9:00–9:30 AM	Break	N/A

9:30–11:00 AM	Individual Imaginal Exposure	Psychologist
11:00–1:00 PM	Group In Vivo Exposure	Psychologist
1:00–2:00 PM	Community Involvement Lunch	Community Partners
2:00–2:30 PM	Break	N/A
2:30–3:30 PM	Acupuncture	Acupuncturist
3:30–4:00 PM	Break	N/A
4:00–5:00 PM	Family Focus: Individual Session	Psychologist
5:00–5:30 PM	Break	N/A
5:30–6:30 PM	Wellness Program: Gentle Yoga	Yoga Therapist
6:30–8:00 PM	Dinner	N/A

Week 2: Day 9: Thursday

Time	Activity	Provider(s)
6:30–7:45 AM	Breakfast	N/A
7:45–8:00 AM	Check-in	N/A
8:00–8:30 AM	Case Management	Social Worker
8:30–9:30 AM	Wellness Session	Psychologist
9:30–11:00 AM	Individual Imaginal Exposure	Psychologist
11:00–1:00 PM	Group In Vivo Exposure	Psychologist
1:00–1:30 PM	Lunch	N/A
1:30–2:00 PM	Assessment	Clinical Nurse
2:00–3:30 PM	Focus Family Group Session	Psychologist
3:30–4:30 PM	Finance and Careers	Patient Outreach Coordinator

Time	Activity	Provider(s)
4:30–5:30 PM	Relapse Prevention	Psychologist
5:30–6:30 PM	Wellness Program: Gentle Yoga	Yoga Therapist
6:30–8:00 PM	Dinner	N/A

Week 2: Day 10: Friday

Time	Activity	Provider(s)
6:30–7:45 AM	Breakfast	N/A
7:45–8:00 AM	Check-in	N/A
8:00–8:30 AM	Case Management	Social Worker
8:30–9:30 AM	Break	N/A
9:30–11:00 AM	Individual Imaginal Exposure	Psychologist
11:00–12:30 PM	Planned Individual In Vivo Exposure	On Own

12:30–1:30 PM	Patient Practice	Program Team
1:30–2:00 PM	Lunch	N/A
2:00–2:30 PM	Posttreatment Assessments	Program Team
2:30–3:00 PM	Graduation	Veteran Care Team

Team Approach

Critical to the success of the program is the interdisciplinary team approach. This begins with an assessment that includes team discussion of each case, treatment goals, and plan and continues with effective communication across the IOP treatment episode ending with the discharge plan and aftercare management. Frequency of team meetings and huddles may vary by program as long as all members of the treatment team are able to communicate in a timely manner to provide updates on patient progress and next steps. In EHVP, in addition to brief hallway contacts for the most urgent issues, we have a case conference to discuss intakes each week (90 minutes on Monday); two consultation meetings (60–90 minutes on Wednesday and Thursday) that cover each active PE-IOP patient and progress or issues, as well as planning for next week's arrivals; and one 30-minute tape-watching consultation (on Monday). Information technology tools may be used to support this communication with consideration for patient privacy. We know that many programs may not allow for this much consultation time, but ensuring that there is adequate team communication is critical to providing truly collaborative care and successful intervention.

During PE-IOP, imaginal exposure sessions are conducted daily with an individual therapist. Group in vivo exposure sessions are conducted by IOP staff. Daily updates of progress in both treatment components support effective treatment and team communication for patient care. Group leaders and individual therapists work closely with case managers and other IOP team members to set up and work through the logistics of in vivo and other exposure exercises that are part of the treatment plan.

Combining group and individual formats provides the strengths that come from group goal setting, cohesion, and social connection while avoiding the drawbacks of individual trauma processing in group.

Missed Sessions

For patients who missed a session due to illness (patient or provider) or other reasons, therapists should work with the patient to increase his review of the imaginal exposure recording and plan for additional in vivo exposures to keep the patient working toward goals as much as possible. Discussion of whether the reason for the missed session will continue or only occur this single time is warranted to prevent additional missed sessions. If circumstances have changed and the patient is no longer able to stay in the program and focus on PTSD for the duration of PE-IOP, then considering modification of the treatment plan to have him return at a different time may be warranted. The outcome we most want to avoid is for a patient to think or feel that he completed the program and did not respond when in fact he did not engage in the program enough to even know if it may be effective for him.

For missed group sessions, the group therapists are immediately in touch with the treatment team to discuss how to remediate the missed psychoeducation or in vivo exposure. For psychoeducation, this most often involves the individual therapist having the psychoeducation discussion with the patient in individual session. If an in vivo exposure was missed, the patient and treatment team should consider either planning for an in vivo exposure with treatment team support staff during alternate hours or planning for the patient to make up the missed in vivo exposure with a planned independent in vivo exposure. All program staff are trained in the overall exposure model and can work with patients as needed to support the idea of approaching the memory and staying with it until it gets less intense and PTSD is reduced.

Alternatively, if a provider (for any of the components) is unavailable due to illness or planned absence, a back-up provider who has worked with the patient should provide the session content to prevent missed sessions.

Cohorts

While not required, the EHVP model uses a partially open rolling-cohort model. Specifically, each Monday, a new group of patients arrives for the 2-week program. Thus, on-site patients consist of those in their first week sharing the group PE-IOP content with those in their second week. This provides an excellent opportunity for new patients to see the progress of patients in week 2 and receive support from those patients. Conversely, patients in week 2 can note how far they have come and serve in a mentoring role that for many is quite reinforcing of what they have learned in PE-IOP. In cases where a patient is interfering with the progress of other patients in group, the treatment team may consider removing the patient from groups and providing some programming individually or potentially sending the patient home due to noncompliance with behavioral expectations.

Staffing

Many different staffing models are currently in use with PE-IOP. Staffing may be influenced by some of the variations discussed in Chapter 8 with regard to what components are provided in addition to the core of exposure. In most programs, the individual imaginal exposure is provided by the same licensed mental health provider for the duration of the program. This person is typically a social worker or psychologist but may be another licensed provider credentialed in psychotherapy. As previously mentioned, providers for the group in vivo and individual imaginal exposure sessions should have PE provider status or be in training for PE provider status. Some programs rotate providers based on scheduling and availability. For these programs, standardized notes that summarize each session content allow providers to pick up across patients without interrupting patient progress.

For all other components, providers should have the proper credentialing and training to support provision of the intervention. For instance, only those providers trained as yoga instructors should provide yoga. Only those instructors trained in CBT for substance use should provide those components.

We will present more detail on the exposure components in Chapter 4.

Patient Materials and Binders

To ease patient and provider communication, patients are provided a copy of the patient workbook (*Reclaiming Your Life from a Traumatic Experience WORKBOOK*, Second Edition; Rothbaum, Foa, Hembree, & Rauch, 2019) and all materials required for the duration of the IOP program. All handouts also appear in Appendix A of this therapist guide. They are also given program-specific behavioral expectations and any logistics information (what to do in an emergency, where to find food, fun things to do in free time, etc.) at check-in on Day 1 in a personal binder. The format and contents of these binders will vary with the specifics of the program but should include at a minimum

1. *Behavioral expectations* with sign-off to remind patients of program requirements and services. See Handout 19: Behavioral Expectations Document (Example) in Appendix A of this guide for an example that can be modified for your program.
2. *All PE-related patient-facing forms* (Handouts 1–4, 6–11, 13, and 15, found in Appendix A), with enough copies for homework completion. Providers should have extra copies as well in case patients forget or lose forms or if patients do more homework than is expected.
3. *All forms for integrative services.*

Patients are asked to carry the binders with them throughout the program, and providers will refer to the binders as patients progress. At the end of the program, patients will be encouraged to retain their binders for future reference. For patients who have continued work, binders will continue to be useful. For patients who have remitted or who no longer need to work on exposures, having the information in their binders may be useful in times of stress or if symptoms return in the future to help maintain gains.

CHAPTER 4   Exposure in PE-IOP

Both imaginal and in vivo exposures are key components in the Prolonged Exposure-Intensive Outpatient Program (PE-IOP). The rationale, structure, and logistics are consistent with standard PE. PE-IOP takes advantage of massed exposures and uses group dynamics to increase patient motivation and speed progress. For efficiency and group cohesion, most of the psychoeducation and in vivo exposure occurs in group sessions. To maximize individual emotional processing and maximize individual imaginal exposure time, imaginal exposure is provided in individual sessions.

Group In Vivo Exposure

The current program builds on the group prolonged exposure model presented in Smith et al. (2015). Group therapists begin in the initial session building an atmosphere of group cohesion to assist in facilitating exposures. You can accomplish this goal by setting up clear expectations for patients to attend all sessions and be respectful of all group members. The first session provides an initial overview rationale for emotional processing theory of posttraumatic stress disorder (PTSD) and how exposure works. It also provides opportunities for group members to share personal experiences of the impact of PTSD symptoms on their lives. Focus the discussion on the most common symptoms to provide a foundation for connection between group members and provide encouragement to share successes and challenges. Similarly to how the presentation of the rationale in standard PE is a discussion rather than a lecture between therapist and patient in individual sessions, PE-IOP group in vivo discussion is intended to present didactic content through a group discussion that touches on the main points of the rationale and connects to the personal experience of each group member. Ideal group size is 6–8 but may range from a low of 4 members to a high of 10 members. All groups are co-led to provide the opportunity for one group therapist to work individually with patients who require more attention.

Two group therapists co-lead the group in vivo sessions, alternating between leading the discussion and walking around the room to monitor that all members are engaged and involved in the session content. If a patient is struggling, one of the group therapists can determine whether the problem should be addressed with the group together—as when the issue may be something that others are concerned about—or whether the group therapist should pull the patient out to work with her individually. In cases of patients who do not follow behavioral expectations, pulling the patient out for corrective action to address noncompliance with behavioral expectations can allow the group to continue without interruption. Once the sessions involve in vivo exposure practice, the two group therapists provide flexibility to split the group into two smaller groups working on different in vivo exposure items (i.e., one therapist takes four people to a "farmers market" exposure, while the other therapist takes the other four patients on a "riding in a car on roads with potholes" exposure). In planning for in vivo exposures, the group therapists typically want to have the first in vivo completed in group to offer the chance for corrective feedback from a therapist. Once patients have a grasp on staying in the situation without engaging in safety behaviors until anxiety decreases, then we encourage moving to independent exposures so that patients can feel in control and empowered to accomplish the items. Additional details on group in vivo sessions are provided in the session-by-session details later in the chapter.

Individual Imaginal Exposure

Imaginal exposure is conducted in individual sessions that start on Day 2. As the core component of PE intervention, imaginal exposure sessions (each 90 minutes) are conducted daily on weekdays during the 2 weeks of IOP. In addition, patients are instructed to listen to the imaginal recording at least once each day during the day. If for some reason an individual session needs to be skipped (due to patient or therapist illness or some other reason), the team first tries to work around rescheduling the session for another time in the same day. If this is not possible, the therapist discusses this with the patient. They then decide, based on the needs of the patient, whether she can listen to the imaginal exposure tape of the previous session additional times to ensure that the exposure is not missed or meet with another provider to complete the session. A phone check-in may also be used to provide the opportunity for processing and to ensure progress continues.

All imaginal exposures (i.e., revisiting the traumatic memory in imagination and recounting it aloud) are conducted as consistent with Foa, Hembree, Rothbaum, and Rauch (2019).

Therapist Note

Throughout this guide, we refer to "the trauma" or "the traumatic event." Please use the words that your patient uses to refer to this event, for example, "the assault," "when Jones was killed," or "the accident."

Some patients comment that they have tried and failed to face their trauma-related fears and other negative emotions or that they did face them, but their distress did not diminish. Some just cannot picture themselves stopping their avoidance or being strong enough to visualize and describe traumatic memories. Others think that avoidance is an effective coping technique, and they need to be encouraged to try another technique. For patients who doubt the efficacy of the treatment or their ability to benefit from it, you should aim to help them see that the approach at least makes sense and that it will be different from how they have approached it in the past. In IOP this may be more common as most patients presenting for IOP have already tried other forms of PTSD treatment and either had difficulty completing them or have not fully responded.

Now that an initial overview of the structure of exposure has been presented, Table 4.1 provides a detailed exposure schedule outline on session-by-session implementation. The descriptions that follow include detailed session outlines of what is to be accomplished (with suggested time frames), the information to convey to your patient, the techniques you will use and how to use them, and what homework to assign to your patient. You may photocopy handouts from this therapist guide

Table 4.1 Exposure therapy daily schedule outline

Day 1 (Monday)
Group In Vivo Exposure Session 1 (2 hours)
▪ Review PTSD symptoms (30 minutes) and treatment rationale with analogy (30 minutes);
▪ Begin creating in vivo hierarchy (50 minutes)
▪ [There is no imaginal exposure therapy on Day 1.]
Day 2 (Tuesday)
Individual Imaginal Exposure Session 1 (90 minutes)
▪ First imaginal exposure and processing
Group In Vivo Exposure Session 2 (2 hours)
▪ Finalize and expand in vivo hierarchy (25 minutes)
▪ Select items and complete exposure exercise individually or in group (70 minutes)
Day 3 (Wednesday)
Individual Imaginal Exposure Session 2 (90 minutes)
▪ Conduct imaginal exposure (60 minutes) and processing (15 minutes)
Group In Vivo Exposure Session 3 (2 hours)
▪ Plan and complete in vivo exposure (65 minutes)
▪ Discuss safety behaviors and address avoidance during in vivo exposure (25 minutes)
Day 4 (Thursday)
Individual Imaginal Exposure Session 3 (90 minutes)
▪ Introduce and conduct hot spots (60 minutes) and processing (15 minutes)
Group In Vivo Exposure Session 4 (2 hours)

Day 5 (Friday), Day 6 (Monday), Day 7 (Tuesday), and Day 8 (Wednesday)

Individual Imaginal Exposure Sessions 4–7 (90 minutes)

▪ Hot spots and processing (15 minutes)

Group In Vivo Exposure Session 5–8 (2 hours)

Day 9 (Thursday)

Individual Imaginal Exposure Session 8 (90 minutes)

▪ Hot spots and processing (15 minutes)

Group In Vivo Exposure Session 9 (1 hour)

▪ Review Homework (10 minutes)

▪ Review in vivo exposure progress and items that need more work (25 minutes)

▪ Discuss relapse prevention (20 minutes)

▪ Farewells (5 minutes)

Day 10 (Friday)

Individual Imaginal Exposure Session 9 (90 minutes)

▪ Entire memory and processing (15 minutes)

▪ Termination/planning for after IOP

Planned Self-Directed In Vivo Exposure (2 hours)

(Appendix A) or download them from the Treatments ThatWork Web site at www.oxfordclinicalpsych.com/PE-IOP.

Additional session-by-session details of how the memory is approached throughout PE-IOP are provided later.

Session 1: Group In Vivo Exposure (2 Hours)

Materials Needed

▪ Dry erase or other device to record group discussion in real time (Smart Board, etc.)

▪ Binder with Session Handouts (see Appendix A in this guide: Handout 1: Rationale for Treatment by Prolonged Exposure; Handout 2: Subjective Units of Distress & In Vivo Exposure Hierarchy; Handout 3: Common Reactions to Trauma; and Handout 4: List of Things to Take Back)

▪ Session Checklist (see Appendix B in this guide)

Session Outline

▪ Review PTSD symptoms (30 minutes) and treatment rationale with analogy (20 minutes)

▪ Create Subjective Units of Distress Scale (SUDS) (10 minutes)

▪ Create in vivo hierarchy (50 minutes)

▪ Assign homework (10 minutes)

Review PTSD Symptoms (30 Minutes) and Treatment Rationale with Analogy (20 Minutes)

Discussion of PTSD begins with a brainstorm exercise to help participants adjust to the group setting and engage with content. This will assist in facilitating understanding of the rationale when presented after group members have identified ways in which avoidance is present in their lives.

The group therapist begins by stating:

What are some of the symptoms or problems that people may have when they have experienced a trauma?

The therapist then writes (where all group participants can see on the white board or other tool) the symptoms and comorbid problems that group members provide. If group members fail to provide examples of symptoms of PTSD—such as intrusions, emotional or physiological responses to triggers, avoidance, or hyperarousal symptoms—the group therapists should facilitate discussion of these symptoms. If possible, limit this to 10 minutes, depending on the responses from the members. The therapist then continues:

> *What kinds of things do you think you avoid because it makes you feel anxious or uneasy or reminds you of your trauma?*

List as many of these situations, people, or places as you can on the white board. If possible, limit this to 10 minutes, depending on the responses from the members. Discuss the items and how they fit with the emotional processing model of PTSD.

Present the rationale for in vivo exposure.

> *Most people have PTSD symptoms after a trauma. But some people recover and others do not, largely due to three factors: (1) avoidance of thinking about the trauma, (2) avoiding situations that remind them of the trauma, and (3) the negative thoughts about what the trauma means about the person and their world.*

Review the reason why avoidance functions to maintain and eventually increase PTSD symptoms. Cover each of the following points and include group interaction and discussion. The following discussion is an example of how this might go.

- Fear and anxiety are easily triggered by trauma reminders.
- Trauma and PTSD can make us feel incompetent and feel that the world is dangerous.
- People with PTSD try to avoid emotions, people, places, and things that remind them of trauma because they are upsetting.
- Avoidance makes sense in the short run but limits choices and life in the long run.
- We will be using two techniques to address avoidance: imaginal and in vivo exposure.

Exposure works by:

- Changing the habit of reducing anxiety or distress by avoidance or escape;
- Staying with the emotion that the trauma memory brings up so that it gets less intense through habituation;

- Disconfirming the belief that anxiety and other negative emotions continue forever;
- Allowing disconfirmation that an avoided situation and traumatic memory are harmful or dangerous; and
- Increasing confidence that we can handle distress.

Discussion then moves to an analogy to illustrate how the treatment works. Here is an example of how you may present this material:

One way that many people deal with feelings of fear or anxiety or other negative emotions is avoidance. They might try to avoid people, places, or things that remind them of what happened. They may also try to push out thoughts or feelings that they have about what happened. This is a way that people try to protect themselves from the thoughts or feelings that remind them of the trauma that may feel overwhelming for them. As we have talked about before, avoidance is very common for people after experiencing a trauma.

As you know, doing things to avoid thinking about uncomfortable memories makes sense in the short term, but it prevents you from:

- *Learning that these memories are not dangerous.*
- *Learning that you can handle the discomfort that your memories may cause.*
- *Seeing that the discomfort you experience decreases the more you confront these memories.*
- *Learning that these emotions belong with the memory, not your current life.*
- *Being able to place your uncomfortable memories into the context of the rest of your life story.*

The group therapists now present an analogy to represent PTSD and how exposure therapy works to treat PTSD. The analogy of the closet is one alterative; the book and the file cabinet (presented in the individual imaginal exposure session on p. 62) are other alternatives.

Until now, your uncomfortable traumatic memories have been like a messy closet. Whenever something reminds you of your trauma, the door of the closet falls open and the most upsetting parts of your memories pop out and fall on the floor. You may start to look at the stuff that fell out, but then feel overwhelmed and shove it all back

*in the closet and slam the closet door closed. Then, the next time
something reminds you of the trauma, the closet door opens again and
the whole process starts over, leaving you feeling out of control. Because
you respond to the memories by slamming the door to push them out
of your mind, you are never really able to see how all of the contents of
your closet fit together and how the scary pieces relate to all the rest of
the stuff.*

*This program is designed to help you approach uncomfortable
memories so that you can learn to control them rather than let the
memories control you. Approaching the memories is like cleaning
out the closet. Instead of shoving things in and closing the door,
you can organize the memories just as you would organize a messy
closet. You can figure out what goes where and why. You can decide
what to keep and what to throw away. By going through each
memory from beginning to end with repetition, you can see how
it all fits together. Also, the more you go over the memories, the
emotions that are connected to them will get less intense. This does
not mean that you will not think about the trauma sometimes, but
that, when you do think about it, it does not bring up all of the
strong emotions. You can feel in control even when you think about
these memories.*

Create Subjective Units of Distress Scale (SUDS) (10 Minutes)

Group therapists work with patients to create the SUDS through a
group discussion, with one therapist leading the discussion and the
other walking around to answer one-on-one questions and review the
progress of the patients.

*As we were just discussing, this treatment involves approaching
instead of avoiding the trauma memory and things associated with
the trauma. Before we start doing that, we need to have a consistent
language for you to convey how much distress you are feeling as you
do this. We call it the Subjective Units of Distress Scale or SUDS. It
is a scale from 0 to 100. [Write the scale on the board and distribute
Handout 2: Subjective Units of Distress & In Vivo Exposure
Hierarchy.]*

As you see on the sheet, there is space for writing down items by the numbers 0, 25, 50, 75, and 100. These are your anchors. I want you to write down a situation for each anchor that is personal for you and things that will not change over time. For example, a time or a place in which you felt totally relaxed might be a 0 on our scale. When you pick an item for an anchor, it should be specific— not an abstract or hypothetical situation. This means a situation like "the first dinner on the beach on my honeymoon" not "the beach." It should not be something you are going to work on. [Instruct group members to do this for each 25-point interval and have them write down a personal example for each.]

0———————25———————50———————75———————100

   0 = no distress/negative affect/totally relaxed;
  25 = not quite relaxed but not distressed;
  50 = beginning to feel negative affect/distress, but it is
       manageable;
  75 = noticeable distress/negative affect with physiological signs;
 100 = the most distress/negative affect you have ever experienced
       in your life

This is the scale that you are going to use to rate how distressed you feel while doing each of your homework assignments. You can choose any number between 0 and 100 when you are recording your SUDS rating. When you do your in vivo exposures, you record your SUDS at the beginning, at the end, and the highest SUDS that you reach during the situation.

Review the anchors of each patient to ensure that they are specific situations and not items that will need to be addressed in treatment. For instance, while a patient may use her target trauma for the 100 anchor, be clear that this is her memory of how she felt *in the moment of the trauma* and *not* how she feels when thinking about the trauma now. We expect how patients feel *now* about the trauma to change as they process the memory in treatment, but the memory of how they felt during the trauma will remain and can be an anchor.

Create In Vivo Hierarchy (50 Minutes)

The group therapists then move on to creating a hierarchy beginning with a brief discussion of the cost of avoidance using the examples provided and recorded on the board during the previous discussion of PTSD.

> *Most of our work in these groups will focus on taking back your life from PTSD through in vivo exposures and practice. You have all shared with us some things that you avoid. What do you think avoiding the things that we have on the board costs you?*

Encourage the group to identify the cost of avoidance, including:

- not able to do what they want to do,
- feelings incompetent to handle difficult situations or emotions,
- conflict in relationships,
- reduction in physical health,
- negative impact on education/occupation,
- mental health issues, and
- increased substance use.

Write on the board the costs that the group members generate, and then move on to a list of people, places, and situation that they want to take back from PTSD.

> *Since we know the cost of avoidance, let's start thinking of situations that you want to stop avoiding. I want you to think of some specific situations, people, places, or activities that you might want to take back from PTSD. On the board, we already have some situations that you are avoiding. What are some other specific situations or activities that you would like to stop avoiding? From your binder, take out Handout 4: List of Things to Take Back, and write down the items that fit for you that are on the board, either those that are already written or those that we add now.*

List on the board the situations that the group members generate. Ensure that all members have a chance to contribute to items on the board. There is not a requirement for how many items each group member contributes. Since this is the first active treatment group, some members may be hesitant. Note these patterns and ensure that the individual therapy providers are aware and available to discuss why and to assist with in vivo hierarchy in their session if needed. While recording all items, group therapists should attend to those items that can be feasibly completed in the current IOP setting. You can be creative in how to problem-solve ways to do in vivo exposures that therapeutically approach the patients' feared consequences.

Consider how the other program elements may provide opportunities for exposures based on each patient's hierarchy. For instance, being a passenger in a vehicle—rather than being the driver—may be on a patient's hierarchy. If this is the case, then ensuring that the participant is recording each ride to receive her pain management acupuncture session as an in vivo exposure creates more opportunity for exposure. Add items such as these if not mentioned and if they seem appropriate for group members:

- being in open areas/tree lines,
- talking about combat/deployment,
- reading the news about combat or conflicts,
- standing in line,
- going to the grocery store,
- sitting in the middle at a movie theatre,
- sitting with one's back to the entrance,
- being in crowded places,
- going to fireworks,
- experiencing movement/people behind them,
- being in places with only one exit,
- attending sporting events,
- sitting in traffic on the interstate,
- going to the mall,
- taking hikes,
- swimming,
- exercising in public place,
- talking to a man,
- signing up for a dating app, and
- driving.

Discuss how anxiety/distress can increase or decrease based on small changes in specific details, like time of day (walking outside when it is dark in a relatively safe area may create more anxiety/distress than when walking in the same place during the day), how many people are around (going to Walmart at noon on a weekday may be easier than on a Saturday afternoon when it is crowded), type of terrain (a road with potholes may be more difficult than a newly paved road), and so on. Explain how one area of avoidance (such as driving) can have many different types of exposures with varying levels of difficulty (driving during the day or at night, driving on a six-lane highway versus a two-lane road, being the driver rather than the passenger, driving on trash day versus another day, driving under overpasses, and driving over bridges).

As the hierarchies are being created on Handout 4, group therapists should present a discussion of relative risk and how items on the hierarchy should generally be things that most people would do and feel are relatively safe. In this initial session, we are only looking for a few items as the patients will be growing the hierarchy as part of their homework. As a guide, if the patient can provide about 5–7 items, she is on the right track. In addition, some people can consider what others in their neighborhood or community do on a regular basis or what they feel they need or want to be able to do in their life. Risk *is* relative, and we cannot guarantee safety to anyone at any time. In vivo exposure is about being able to do the things participants want to do to have a quality of life that works for them.

> *Now looking at the list that we made: What might other people think about engaging in these activities? What would you say is the relative level of risk for these situations? What do you think about the safety level?*
>
> *Initially, the situations that you identified may feel like they are dangerous. This is PTSD. At the time of your trauma or shortly after, these things got paired with danger. So, these items feel dangerous because of what happened in the past. However, for those things we put on the list, your sense of danger is more than it needs to be NOW. By approaching and staying in these situations, even with some anxiety, you can reset what feels dangerous and take these choices back from PTSD.*

Of note, the discussion in the group will focus on what has been presented to the group on the white board. Some patients may not share all of their items with the group, and this may be appropriate. The group therapists should be mingling through the group to touch base with each member on an individual basis at least briefly, to ensure each is grasping the task and creating a reasonable list.

Assign Homework (10 Minutes)

▪ Instruct the patients to expand on their individual hierarchy for homework using Handout 2: Subjective Units of Distress & in Vivo Exposure Hierarchy. In addition, ask them to read Handout 1: Rationale for Treatment by Prolonged Exposure and Handout 3: Common Reactions to Trauma, and encourage patients to share the sheets with significant others as appropriate.

Day 2

Session 1: Individual Imaginal Exposure (90 Minutes)

Materials Needed

▪ Recording device (PE coach, smartphone, or other digital recording method)
▪ Binder with Session Handouts (see Appendix A in this guide: Handout 15: Example of Blank PE-IOP Goal Sheet and Handout 6: Imaginal Exposure Homework Recording Form)
▪ Handout 5: Therapist Imaginal Exposure Recording Form
▪ Session Checklist (see Appendix B in this guide)

Session Outline

▪ Present individual session goals and rationale for imaginal exposure (15 minutes)
▪ Present directions and conduct imaginal exposure (45 minutes) and processing (15 minutes)
▪ Assign homework (5 minutes)

Present Individual Session Goals and Rationale for Imaginal Exposure (15 Minutes)

Review the patient's goals from Handout 15: Example of Blank PE-IOP Goal Sheet, completed in case management prior to coming to the PE-IOP (see Chapter 5). If the goals do not fit PE work, then work with the patient to find PE-specific goals. Explain how this treatment will address the patient's PTSD symptoms by focusing on those changes that are most important to this patient.

Therapist Note

Breathing retraining is not included in PE-IOP in many models, including the Emory Healthcare Veterans Program (EHVP) model. This is the case because imaginal exposure begins on Day 2, and preference is to have all homework time spent listening to the imaginal exposure tape rather than split between breathing retraining and the memory. In rare circumstances, breathing retraining may be introduced later for patients who are over-engaging with the memory in session or when listening to their imaginal exposure recording. In recognition that some programs use this technique, it is covered in Chapter 8 as a variation, and Handout 18: Breathing Retraining Technique is included in Appendix A.

The therapist reviews the overall rationale that was presented in the group session on Day 1. The rationale for imaginal exposure includes the following five points:

1. Processing and organizing the memory
2. Promoting differentiation between "remembering" the traumatic event and "being retraumatized"
3. Promoting reduction of distress
4. Promoting the realization that talking and thinking about the trauma does not cause the patient to go crazy or fall apart
5. Increasing mastery and sense of control

Example discussion is provided here.

> *Remember from group that two factors that maintain PTSD over time are avoidance and negative thoughts about yourself and the world. As we discussed in group, avoidance sometimes works in the short run, but, in the long run, it prevents you from learning that you*

can handle the memory. Confronting it is difficult but not dangerous. Remembering is uncomfortable but does not mean it is happening again. You can handle the distressing feelings connected to the memory, and these feelings become less intense if you stay with them. Finally, by approaching instead of avoiding, you learn that those intense feelings do not last forever and you do not go crazy. In approaching the memory you can also consider new ways to think about the trauma and what it says about you and the world.

Imagine that your traumatic event is recorded in your brain like a book, with paragraphs, pages, and sections. Like all books, your traumatic event book is a story with a beginning, middle, and end. Because you try to avoid thinking about your trauma, you have not read the book from the beginning to the end since the trauma occurred. Whenever you have a flashback or distressing memory, the book is opened automatically at the paragraph where the flashback is written and you read this paragraph. Reading this part of the book is painful and distressing. So you say to yourself, "I don't like this book," and with some effort you manage to close the book. The same thing happens when you have the next flashback or thought about your trauma. And this is why you have not read what is written in the book. In imaginal exposure, we will read the book together from the beginning to the end. This will give you an opportunity to view the traumatic event and its meaning from your perspective today, rather than from the perspective of the past when the trauma happened and you felt terrified [or "so ashamed" or "terribly guilty"].

Present Directions and Conduct Imaginal Exposure (45 Minutes) and Processing (15 Minutes)

Therapist and patient discuss the index trauma (the trauma that is bringing up the most distress at the present, the trauma that haunts the patient the most or that elicits more intrusions and flashbacks than other traumas) and determine the beginning and end of the index trauma event. The beginning is typically the moment when the patient felt something was going wrong. This start may be refined based on the patient's response during imaginal exposure. The end is the moment when she felt she was in less danger or relatively safe.

Present the directions, including:

- Recount the trauma aloud with your eyes closed from beginning to end in the present tense.
- Visualize as though it is happening now and include all thoughts, feelings, and other details.
- When we get to the end, we will repeat it for the time we have today.
- I will ask for SUDS about every 5 minutes. When I do, just throw out a number between 0 and 100 of how you feel right now, sitting here in this office with me.
- I am going to make a recording of this imaginal exposure, and I want you to listen to the recording at least once per day between sessions.

Imaginal Exposure Information for the Therapist

Imaginal exposure, or revisiting the trauma memory in imagination, is a procedure in which the patient is asked to visualize and emotionally connect with the traumatic event while recounting the experience aloud, in the present tense. Imaginal exposure is not a conversation between you and the patient. The standard procedure is designed to

- Enhance the patient's ability to access all of the salient aspects of the trauma memory: details about the event, thoughts, emotions, and sensory experiences.
- Promote emotional engagement with the trauma memory.
- Invite narration of the memory in the patient's own words with minimal direction and prompting by the therapist.

Allow the patient to approach the trauma memory gradually the first time she revisits and recounts it. In general, do not be too directive when the patient describes the trauma experience or ask too many questions in this first exposure. It is important that the patient be in control of the process of remembering the trauma and the feelings associated with it. Therefore, give the patient permission to approach the memories at her own pace and provide a calm and supportive presence.

Patients are sometimes reluctant to engage fully with the emotional aspects of recounting the trauma memory. Remember, while anxiety is often a focus in PTSD treatment, any negative affect that the patient experienced at the time of the trauma or subsequently should be included. During the first imaginal revisiting (exposure) of the trauma memory, the patient should be allowed to determine the level of detail with which she recounts the narrative of her trauma with minimal interruption from you. In subsequent repetitions and sessions, encourage her to provide more details about the trauma and to engage with the emotional content of the memory more fully through probes for more details about the event as well as the emotional, cognitive, and physiological reactions that occurred during the trauma. It is typical that the first imaginal exposures may not include the level of detail we encourage in later sessions, and this is okay.

Prolonged or Multiple-Incident Traumas

For patients with a prolonged trauma (e.g., a period of torture, several days of captivity), or multiple incident traumas (e.g., repeated assaults, recurring childhood sexual abuse, multiple incidents of combat), you will need to establish which of the traumatic memories will be the focus of imaginal exposure. Usually start with "the worst or the first." Typically, these are the memories that are the most intrusive and distressing at the present time. It may also be the first (e. g., first incident of incest, first enemy fire in combat). In most cases, successful processing of the most disturbing memory will generalize to less distressing memories so that they, too, will become less distressing. Sometimes, even after processing the most distressing memory, another traumatic experience continues to trigger high levels of distress. In this case, proceed to using imaginal exposure with that memory after the first memory is much less distressing. We include more detail on conducting imaginal exposure later in the chapter.

Processing

After the imaginal revisiting of the trauma memory, you will process the experience with the patient for approximately 15–30 minutes. In brief, processing involves encouraging the patient to talk about her reactions to revisiting the trauma memory and to discuss feelings and thoughts that she may have about the trauma or its meaning in her life. The process of imaginal recounting of the trauma memory creates powerful opportunities for learning. It is common for patients to emerge from imaginal (and in vivo) exposure with new awareness or insights. Asking the patient to describe and expand on these insights makes them more explicit, and she often begins to reevaluate and modify unrealistic views or expectations.

Processing begins with encouragement for any memory approach that the patient has attempted or completed followed by review of SUDS patterns and a discussion of how it felt for the participant today, either in contrast to her expectations or previous experience. Always use short, open-ended questions with a reflective and noninterpretive style. Focus on what the patient brings up either during the imaginal exposure or the processing. Allow the patient to present her observations first. Periods of silence can be helpful if the patient is considering her experience or thoughts. This can be part of good processing. For example:

> *You did a great job. How was it for you to revisit the memory today? (Pause.) Was it harder or easier than you expected? (Pause.) What thoughts and feelings did you notice? (Pause.) Was there anything new that you hadn't thought about in a while?*

Initially questions may be about her reaction.

> *What did you notice in the second or third retelling today?*

If the patient does not bring up a topic to discuss, use the information that you learned while listening to the patient's recounting of the traumatic memory and ask for clarification. For example:

> *I noticed that you said several times that you could have saved your friend and did not. Tell me more about that?*

It is important that the patient not leave the session in great distress or with high anxiety. Plan treatment sessions so that there will be sufficient time at the end of the session to help the patient alleviate her distress level. It is also helpful to tell the patient that she may temporarily feel more upset after some imaginal exposure sessions, especially the early ones, and relief after others. Finally, it may also be helpful to tell the patient that anxiety and distress during imaginal recounting of the trauma memory reflect the beginning of emotional processing of the distressing memories (i.e., the beginning of healing from the trauma). Remind the patient that the whole PE-IOP team can assist as needed to help her continue to approach the memory.

Assign Homework (5 Minutes)

- Instruct the patient to listen to the imaginal exposure recording at least once and record SUDS on Handout 6: Imaginal Exposure Homework Recording Form.

Day 2

Session 2: Group In Vivo Exposure (2 Hours)

Materials Needed

- Dry erase or other device to record group discussion in real time (Smart Board, etc.)
- Binder with Session Handouts (see Appendix A in this guide: Handout 2: Subjective Units of Distress & In Vivo Exposure Hierarchy; Handout 7: Gradual Exposure; and Handout 8: In Vivo Exposure Homework Recording Form)
- Session Checklist (see Appendix B in this guide)

Session Outline

- Review homework (10 minutes)
- Expand in vivo hierarchy (30 minutes)
- Select items and complete exposure exercise individually or in group (75 minutes)
- Assign homework (5 minutes)

Review Homework (10 Minutes)

Group therapists review thoughts and questions from the rationale and last session, and they review lists of things to take back from PTSD.

Expand In Vivo Hierarchy (30 Minutes)

Yesterday, using Handout 4, you created a list of things you want to take back from PTSD. This will become your hierarchy. [Direct participants to Handout 2: Subjective Units of Distress & In Vivo Exposure Hierarchy.]

Try to put at least 10 items on your hierarchy. Keep in mind that this is YOUR treatment plan and you will determine what you do and do not do each day. There may be items that seem too difficult, but I challenge you to add them to the list and then talk with your treatment team about how and when to approach them. Taking on difficult situations and finding ways to gradually approach and work on them in steps is a BIG part of what we do as exposure therapists, and we are happy to help you think through the tough situations. Your case managers will discuss logistics as well in their daily meetings with you. We suggest that you begin to gradually confront these situations like you would learning how to ride a bike with training wheels, then moving up the training wheels, and then taking off the training wheels. Let's look at this as climbing up steps to get to your goal.

Draw steps on the board, and choose one of the homework assignments for an example to break down the in vivo exposure into gradual steps. Then review the idea of graded exposures, including taking a buddy or coach along for the first few tries. Next, the group leader directs the patients to pull Handout 7: Gradual Exposure, out of their binders.

Are there ways that you can break your hierarchy items into steps to help you reach your goal? Add items to your hierarchy for these steps. Look at your hierarchy and rate any items that you have not already rated. [Provide time for rating and proceed when the group is ready.] Now that you have your SUDS for all those items, we will refer to this list as your hierarchy for the next 2 weeks [or 3 weeks if the program is longer]. Does anyone want to change the items on the list? Let's spend the next few minutes considering this plan, and raise your hand for assistance if you want to talk through your list with one of us. There may be important situations that are hard to do in the IOP. If you are wondering about a situation that you think is important to work on but you are not sure how to approach it, please let us know and we can talk it through with you. Believe me, you are probably not alone.

As group members are making these ratings and refining their hierarchy on Handout 2, the co-therapists are walking around the room and seeing how the members are doing with the task. Provide feedback for both people doing well and for those having trouble. Focus on whether members have a distribution of items and SUDS ratings. Look for issues that need to be addressed. What numbers are people getting? Are anyone's numbers all high for the situations on her list? If they are, direct the patient back to her list to pick one or two situations that are between 40 and 60 on the SUDS or assist her to look for ways to vary the situations to make them more or less difficult. Conversely, if someone only has low items or has several items below 50, suggest that she look back at the list and include situations between 80 and 90 or that she modifies items to increase difficulty. The group therapists then determine what issues in the hierarchy are best handled one-on-one or presented to the group for clarification. Ensure the hierarchies include a spread from 50 to 100 on the SUDS.

Select Items and Complete Exposure Exercise Individually or in Group (75 Minutes)

Now we want each of you to choose the assignment that you are going to do today. We suggest that it is one of the situations that is lower on your hierarchy, at about a 40–50 SUDS. Think of the hierarchy as a ladder. We are going to climb up from the bottom where the exercises are a little easier to the top where the exercises are the hardest. What has everyone chosen for today?

- Write up the in vivo exposures on the board along with the SUDS level for each member while providing encouragement.
- If you determine that a patient is highly anxious, you might consider starting in vivo exposure at a 30–40 SUDS level rather than 40.

For the first in vivo exposure practice in session, try to establish two group exposure exercises and assign patients to go accompanied to complete one of these exposures so that the participant has the experience of doing the in vivo exposure with a group therapist. This most often can involve going to a mall or crowded market situation or sitting in a place where people can be behind you (like a waiting room) without scanning. The group therapists then each take half the patients and walk them through an in vivo exposure to see how they stay in the situation, record SUDS, and repeat it as needed. It is most important that the initial exposure is successful and in the mid-range of SUDS. If the group therapists are not able to fit all patients into two groups for the first exposure, then they provide additional direction as needed, or additional team members may assist to ensure that each patient learns how to do in vivo exposure. Once an initial exposure is done with a group therapist, additional therapist-guided exposures are not usually necessary except in cases of extreme safety behaviors or for patients who are not following through on planned exposures due to avoidance. In such cases, make individual plans to ensure support is provided when needed but is discontinued as soon as possible to allow the patient to experience independent success.

If in vivo group exercises were planned, make sure these are on each patient's hierarchy and rated. Group therapists review guidelines for in vivo exposures, including:

- Stay in the situation for 30 to 45 minutes or until your SUDS rating drops to half its highest level. Leaving the situation while SUDS are high does not provide the opportunity to learn that the emotion can reduce with time.
- Stay present and do not distract yourself.
- Repeat the practice at least once a day. The more you practice, the more you will take this hierarchy item back from PTSD and the more quickly you will see your distress reduced.
- Allow yourself to experience negative emotions that come when you are doing in vivo exposures. Stay with these emotions, and they will decrease with time. If you are not feeling that they are reducing and you are there for the full time, bring this back to the group therapists for discussion. Remember that while in the short term it can cause you to feel an increase in anxiety and distress, in the long term you are taking back control of your life.
- Think of treatment as your full-time job for the next 2 weeks.
- Record your practices and share them with the group.
- Reconvene in the group room after exposure.

Our preference is to use the PE coach app for recording of in vivo exposures, but if that is not possible, use Handout 8: In Vivo Exposure Homework Recording Form. Regardless of the method of collection, ensure that patients know that the in vivo forms are a way for group members to report on their progress in moving up the hierarchy.

Assign Homework (5 Minutes)

■ Prior to the end of session, make sure that each patient has a clear plan for which in vivo exposures she is working on between sessions.

Day 3

Session 2: Individual Imaginal Exposure (90 Minutes)

Materials Needed

■ Devices (PE coach, smartphone, or other digital recording method)
■ Binder with Session Handouts (see Appendix A in this guide: Handout 6: Imaginal Exposure Homework Recording Form)
■ Handout 5: Therapist Imaginal Exposure Recording Form
■ Session Checklist (see Appendix B in this guide)

Session Outline

■ Review homework (10 minutes)
■ Conduct imaginal exposure (60 minutes) and processing (15 minutes)
■ Assign homework (5 minutes)

Review Homework (10 Minutes)

Briefly review imaginal and in vivo homework assignments. Briefly review SUDS and patient experience. If there were problems with in vivo exposure, do not spend too much time discussing these at session start, but make sure to touch base with the patient during processing and inform the in vivo group therapists as needed. Address avoidance or any problems with completing the homework, as consistent with Foa, Hembree, Rothbaum, and Rauch (2019). Give lots of praise for having done whatever she could do, and repeat that confronting the memory is how she can take back control from the memory/PTSD. Problem-solve any issues that may have arisen, and work with the PE-IOP team as needed to support the patient and resolve any problems.

Therapist Note

At every other session (e.g., in sessions 2, 4, 6, 8, and 10), briefly review self-report scales completed during case management with the patient at the beginning of the session. It can be helpful to comment on changes in symptoms as treatment progresses.

Conduct Imaginal Exposure (60 Minutes) and Processing (15 Minutes)

Continue imaginal exposure for up to 60 minutes without interruption. The length of time spent recounting the trauma (or number of repetitions) will often depend on how long patients take to go through their narratives and on their patterns of SUDS levels. In general, try to have the patient repeat the narrative until distress levels decrease. Even if such reduction of distress does not occur within a session, the recounting of the trauma memory should be terminated when sufficient time remains to process the experience with the patient. During processing and homework assignment, the patient's distress will decrease.

Processing continues as described in Individual Session 1 (see pp. 62–66) with increasing focus on the patient's changes in meaning and increased competence.

Assign Homework (5 Minutes)

▪ Instruct the patient to listen to the imaginal exposure recording at least once and record SUDS on Handout 6: Imaginal Exposure Homework Recording Form.

Session 3: Group In Vivo Exposure (2 Hours)

Materials Needed

- Dry erase or other device to record group discussion in real time (Smart Board, etc.)
- Binder with Session Handouts (see Appendix A in this guide: Handout 8: In Vivo Exposure Homework Recording Form) and Handout 9: Safety Behaviors
- Session Checklist (see Appendix B in this guide)

Session Outline

- Review homework (10 minutes)
- Discuss safety behaviors and address avoidance during in vivo exposure (25 minutes)
- Plan and complete in vivo exposure (65 minutes)
- Assign homework (10 minutes)

Review Homework (10 Minutes)

Group therapists begin with a review of the homework, and they record progress on the board for the group.

- Review with each group member the assignment that they chose.
- Discuss the SUDS levels that people reported.
- Identify if individuals experienced habituation.
- Identify problems that people experienced.

Discuss Safety Behaviors and Address Avoidance During In Vivo Exposure (25 Minutes)

Review the concept of safety behaviors in a discussion with group members. Key points to cover include

- Safety behaviors are those that people do or say to provide a temporary reduction of negative emotions in an upsetting situation (e.g., carrying anti-anxiety medication, carrying a gun or a knife, carrying a cell phone at all times, and sleeping with the light on). They are often used by someone with PTSD to reduce the sense of vulnerability to threat in a nonthreatening environment (e.g., in a crowded store).

- Like avoidance, safety behaviors make sense in the short run, but, in the long run, they maintain negative emotions and prevent us from learning that we can handle the situation without the safety behavior and that the threat level is not as high as it feels.

If safety behaviors have already come up in practicing in vivo exposures, those examples can be used in discussion. Not all of the examples here need to be used in any given session as long as the preceding bullet points have been covered.

Now we are going to review a concept called safety behaviors. *What are they? What do you think safety behaviors are? [Write answers on board.] What are some common safety behaviors?*

Write answers on the board and make sure to include the following items if the group does not generate these.

- Scanning the environment for danger ("pulling guard duty")
- Checking for exits and points of escape (e.g., at stores or restaurants)
- Carrying a weapon
- Sitting/standing with your back to the wall or in a corner position
- Checking out a location for safety (e.g., store parking lot) prior to going there to do something you need to do (e.g., shopping)
- Carrying anti-anxiety medication
- Holding keys/cell phone in hand

Group therapists should engage in a discussion about the recognition of social context and cultural variations relevant to safety behaviors, such as checking surroundings and being alert. For instance, scanning when you are in a combat zone is your job and helps you survive. Scanning when you return home and are in church prevents you from engaging with the service and your family. Coverage of relative risks often comes up in group discussion as well. For instance, people who live in higher crime areas have a different level of daily accepted risk and also probably engage in some functional scanning, as would service members on a deployment or police officers on duty. The discussion should highlight the difference between this type of awareness and behaviors related to PTSD in subjectively safe situations. The discussion then connects it to the maintenance of PTSD.

How do safety behaviors maintain PTSD? What do you learn if you do in vivo exposures with safety behaviors? Without safety behaviors?

Following a discussion of safety behaviors, the group reviews avoidance and problem-solves together how to further reduce any avoidance that has come up in the in vivo exposures completed so far. Common issues for discussion include:

▪ If a group member shared that she did not go more than once or left quickly from an in vivo exposure, discuss what happened and how to prevent this from happening again. Make sure to discuss that leaving while distress is high actually can reinforce a sense that the situation is dangerous and that the patient cannot handle it.

▪ If necessary review the treatment rationale, need for practice, and need to remain in the situation long enough for SUDS to decrease.

▪ Decide if one-on-one discussion is needed and implement.

Plan and Complete In Vivo Exposure (65 Minutes)

Ask group members to each choose two situations to work on today. List these situations on the board along with the corresponding SUDS level.

Next, break down each item into specific in vivo exercises. Each patient plans out her in vivo exposure for the day, and group therapists review logistics for these exposures. While the points listed here are the same as discussed in the previous session, the group therapists decide what needs to be emphasized based on group member progress. This discussion may get briefer as patients begin to understand the exercises. Possible discussion points may include

▪ Stay in the situation for 30–45 minutes or until your SUDS rating drops to half its highest level. Leaving the situation while SUDS are high does not provide the opportunity to learn that the emotion can reduce with time.

- Stay present and do not distract yourself.
- Repeat the practice at least once a day. The more you practice, the more you will take this hierarchy item back from PTSD and the more quickly you will see your distress reduced.
- Allow yourself to experience negative emotions that come when you are doing in vivo exposures. Stay with these emotions, and they will decrease with time. If you are not feeling that they are reducing and you are there for the full time, bring this back to the group therapists for discussion. Remember that while, in the short term, it can cause you to feel an increase in anxiety and distress, in the long-term, you are taking back control of your life.
- Think of treatment as your full-time job for the next 2 weeks.
- Record your practices and share them with the group.
- Reconvene in the group room after exposure.

Once the plan is set for each member, they proceed to complete their in vivo exposures in groups or individually and with the therapists or without as appropriate.

Assign Homework (10 Minutes)

- Prior to the end of this session, make sure that each patient has a clear plan for which in vivo exposures she is working on between sessions.
- The group therapists decide whether to meet up to debrief and assign homework for the last 5 minutes of session time or whether patients can move on to the next sessions right from in vivo practice. This decision is based on logistics (can patients come by within the time frame to debrief the in vivo exposure?) and patient progress (if a patient is not following through on exposures on her own, then check-in is indicated).

Sessions 3 Through 7: Individual Imaginal Exposure (90 Minutes)

Materials Needed

- Devices (PE coach, smartphone, or other digital recording method)
- Binder with Session Handouts (see Appendix A in this guide: Handout 6: Imaginal Exposure Homework Recording Form)
- Handout 5: Therapist Imaginal Exposure Recording Form
- Session Checklist (see Appendix B in this guide)

Session Outline

- Review homework (10 minutes)
- Conduct imaginal exposure (60 minutes) and processing (15 minutes)
- Assign homework (5 minutes)

Review Homework (10 minutes)

Briefly review imaginal and in vivo homework assignments. Review SUDS and patient's experience briefly, as in the previous sessions. Address avoidance, provide praise, and problem-solve any issues with completing the homework, as consistent with Foa, Hembree, Rothbaum, and Rauch (2019). Work with the PE-IOP team as needed to support and resolve.

Therapist Note

In Sessions 3–8 (or close to the final session), progressively focus more on "hot spots" as therapy advances. Return to a recounting of the entire memory when anxiety associated with hot spots has sufficiently reduced, but make sure to do so by the final session.

Conduct Imaginal Exposure (60 Minutes) and Processing (15 Minutes)

As in the previous session, continue imaginal exposure for about 60 minutes without interruption.

Beginning at Individual Imaginal Exposure Session 3, emotional processing of the trauma memories can be made more efficient by having the patient focus primarily or exclusively on the most *currently* distressing parts of the trauma, which we term the "hot spots." The hot spots procedure is typically introduced after three sessions of imaginal exposure and distress to the memory has been reduced in general. In the session in which you introduce the hot spots procedure, after homework review, briefly explain to the patient the rationale for hot spots.

> *Now that you are having some reduction in distress to the overall memory, we will begin to work on "hot spots." There are certain points in the memory that hold strong meaning and intense emotional reactions. Often these moments occur when you realized you may be killed or seriously injured or during a moment of important meaning for you. We call these "hot spots." In order to really address these hot spots, we need to slow down the imaginal exposure process and specifically focus in, as if in slow motion, including what you felt, saw, heard, and thought. Just as we have done with the whole memory, we will repeat the hot spot as many times as necessary to "wear it out" or bring about a big decrease in your SUDS level. When that part seems to have been sufficiently processed, we will move to the next one. It is similar to what sometimes happens during a massage, when the massage therapist works on a knot in a muscle over and over until it is smoothed out and then moves to the next knot.*

The patient and you then identify the hot spots on the basis of the patient's self-report of the *currently* most distressing moments of the traumatic event, and you record them on Handout 5: Therapist Imaginal

Exposure Recording Form. If the patient does not identify a part of the memory that in your perception is likely a hot spot (e.g., the part where the patient always gives high SUDS ratings or avoids that part somewhat during the exposure), ask her whether that part is a hot spot as well. Decide together which hot spot would be best to focus on first (typically, most difficult to easiest).

Focus on the patient's hot spots during the imaginal exposure until each has been sufficiently processed, as reflected by diminished SUDS levels and the patient's behavior (e.g., body movement, facial expression). This may take several sessions, depending on the number of hot spots, the patient's pace, and the amount of time she spends listening to exposure recordings as homework. Sometimes a patient gives low SUDS ratings and/or appears minimally distressed even when focusing on a very distressing part of the memory (usually due to underengagement in the trauma memory). In these cases, focusing in on the hot spot and asking the patient to describe this focused portion of the event in detail may increase engagement and SUDS, allowing for a reduction of distress to occur.

If there is more than one trauma memory that is connected to PTSD reexperiencing and avoidance symptoms and that requires processing with imaginal exposure, plan to move to the second memory, allowing enough time for hot spots exposure to fully process both memories. The therapist moves to the second memory after the patient has fully processed the first memory, and the imaginal exposure process remains the same as for the first memory.

When the hot spots work is completed, have the patient return to focusing on and recounting the entire trauma memory, putting it all back together. If there is more than one trauma, this full memory exposure occurs prior to moving to the new memory. If there is just one target trauma memory, this will typically occur in the last session of treatment. Processing continues as described in Individual Session 1 (see pp. 62–66) with increasing focus on the patient's changes in meaning and increased competence.

Assign Homework (5 Minutes)

- Instruct the patient to listen to the imaginal exposure recording at least once and record SUDS on Handout 6: Imaginal Exposure Homework Recording Form.

Days 4 Through 8

Sessions 4 Through 8: Group In Vivo Exposure (2 Hours)

Materials Needed

- Dry erase or other device to record group discussion in real time (Smart Board, etc.)
- Binder with Session Handouts (see Appendix A in this guide: Handout 8: In Vivo Exposure Homework Recording Form)
- Session Checklist (see Appendix B in this guide)

Session Outline

- Review homework (10 minutes)
- Address avoidance during in vivo exposure (10 minutes)
- Plan and complete in vivo exposure (95 minutes)
- Assign homework (5 minutes)

Review Homework (10 Minutes)

Group therapists begin with review of the homework, and they record progress on the board for the group.

- Review with each group member the assignment that they chose.
- Discuss SUDS levels that people reported.
- Identify if individuals experienced habituation.
- Identify problems that people experienced.

Address Avoidance During In Vivo Exposure (10 Minutes)

As in previous sessions, address avoidance during in vivo exposure. This includes exploring the patterns of SUDS in the exposures. If SUDS are reduced, then work should focus on moving up the hierarchy to more difficult items. If SUDS are not reduced, the therapist and patient should focus on whether safety behaviors are present and interfering with habituation. If such behaviors are present, then working on how to reduce or eliminate them should occur.

Plan and Complete In Vivo Exposure (95 Minutes)

As in previous sessions, plan and complete in vivo exposure. This may include individual exposures or groups exposures. Expectations should be high for patients to use the full time allotted for exposures.

Assign Homework (5 Minutes)

- Prior to the end of this session, make sure that each patient has a clear plan for which in vivo exposures she is working on between sessions.
- The group therapists decide whether to meet up to debrief and assign homework for the last 5 minutes of session time or whether patients can move on to the next sessions right from in vivo practice. This decision is based on logistics (can patients come by within the time frame to debrief the in vivo exposure?) and patient progress (if a patient is not following through on exposures on her own, then check-in is indicated).

Day 9

Session 8: Individual Imaginal Exposure (90 Minutes)

Materials Needed

- Devices (PE coach, smartphone, or other digital recording method)
- Binder with Session Handouts (see Appendix A in this guide: Handout 6: Imaginal Exposure Homework Recording Form)

- Handout 5: Therapist Imaginal Exposure Recording Form
- Session Checklist (see Appendix B in this guide)

Session Outline

- Review homework (10 minutes)
- Conduct imaginal exposure (60 minutes) and processing (15 minutes)
- Assign homework (5 minutes)

Review Homework (10 Minutes)

Briefly review imaginal and in vivo homework assignments. Review SUDS and patients experience briefly as in the previous sessions. Address avoidance, provide praise, and problem-solve any issues with completing the homework, as consistent with Foa, Hembree, Rothbaum, and Rauch (2019). Work with the PE-IOP team as needed to support and resolve.

Conduct Imaginal Exposure (60 Minutes) and Processing (15 Minutes)

As in the previous session, continue imaginal exposure for about 60 minutes without interruption, focusing on hotspots. When the hot spots work is completed, have the patient return to focusing on and recounting the entire trauma memory, putting it all back together. This will typically occur in the last session of treatment. Processing continues as described in Individual Session 1 (see pp. 62–66), with increasing focus on patient's changes in meaning and increased competence.

Assign Homework (5 Minutes)

- Instruct the patient to listen to the imaginal exposure recording at least once and record SUDS on Handout 6: Imaginal Exposure Homework Recording Form.

Session 9: Group In Vivo Exposure (1 Hour)

Materials Needed

- Dry erase or other device to record group discussion in real time (Smart Board, etc.)
- Binder with Session Handouts (see Appendix A in this guide: Handout 2: Subjective Units of Distress & In Vivo Exposure Hierarchy; Handout 10: Relapse Prevention Skills; and Handout 11: Managing Stress)
- Session Checklist (see Appendix B in this guide)

Session Outline (Final Session 60 Minutes Only)

- Review homework (10 minutes)
- Review in vivo progress and items that need more work (25 minutes)
- Discuss relapse prevention (20 minutes)
- Farewells (5 minutes)

Review Homework (10 Minutes)

Group therapists begin with review of homework, and they record progress on the board for the group.

- Review with each group member the assignment that she chose.
- Discuss SUDS levels that people reported.
- Identify if individuals experienced habituation.
- Identify problems that people experienced.

Review In Vivo Progress and Items that Need More Work (25 Minutes)

Group therapists use Handout 2: Subjective Units of Distress & In Vivo Exposure Hierarchy to review overall progress on items.

Pull out your in vivo hierarchy (Handout 2). Imagine that you are going out to do each of the items today and rate your SUDS for each. Write your SUDS in the second column.

Allow group members to re-rate their SUDS.

Now, what do you notice about the two columns? Are there items that surprise you? What are two items that have changed the most?

Write on the board the pre-/post-SUDS for two items for each group member. Discuss what the participants think and feel about the changes. Why did SUDS decrease?

Now, which two items did not change as much as you would have liked?

For each group member, write two items on the board with pre-/post-SUDS. Why didn't these SUDS scores decrease?

What are some ways that you can continue using the skills that you have learned to confront these items and help reduce your distress even more?

Assist group members in identifying ways to address these in vivo exposures going forward in their lives. Also ensure that you cover how family members can help support continued exposures.

Discuss Relapse Prevention (20 Minutes)

Group therapists next review and discuss relapse prevention, with a focus on what patients have learned in the group; make sure to cover the following points:

- When you confront rather than avoid the activities, places, people, or things that cause distress or anxiety, negative affect goes down with time.
- You can handle negative affect.
- The negative feelings (such as anxiety or distress) will not last forever.
- These situations are relatively safe.
- You can feel relaxed and don't always have to be on guard.
- You can take control back from anxiety and make your own choices about how you live your life.

What did you learn as you worked through your in vivo exposures?

Write group members' responses on the board and discuss the themes presented, with a focus on those themes that support self-competency, ability to manage negative affect, and approaching the trauma memories and things related to the trauma. Keep this discussion shorter so that you can move to the same question when focused on memory exposure.

Group therapists then review the imaginal exposure pull-out sessions.

> *What did you learn during your individual imaginal sessions when you confronted the memory?*

Write group members' responses on the board. Make sure to cover the major points of the rationale.

- You can handle the memory and the feelings that come with the memory.
- The memory cannot harm you and is not happening now.
- You can think about the memory when you choose, and it does not have control over you.
- Negative feelings will not last forever.

> *What are you going to do if you are feeling the urge to avoid places, situations, people, or thoughts and memories?*

Lead a discussion of the need to confront rather than avoid—often using the idea that avoidance is like weeds in a garden.

> *Think about avoidance as the weeds in your garden. You need to go out and weed the garden to make sure the weeds don't take over. If you notice the weeds of avoidance, you can go out and pull them. This means that if you notice the desire to avoid situations or things, then you need to confront it. If there is a section of your trauma that you didn't confront in treatment, it is like leaving a bunch of weeds in your garden. You need to go pull them out. What things might you be avoiding right now that you need to confront? What do you want to continue to work on when you get home?*

Write group members' responses on the board. Ensure that each group member has at least one and possibly more specific in vivo exposures to work on when they get home.

Then direct patients to Handout 10: Relapse Prevention Skills, for members to write responses.

How are you going to keep using your skills in the future? How are you going to continue to weed your garden?

Discuss ways to continue to use the skills learned in treatment.

Group therapists continue with how to tell the difference between normal life stress and an increase in PTSD symptom(s).

Remember, stress is a normal part of life. You will experience distress, sadness, stress, anxiety, and many other negative emotions in response to things that happen in your life. When you feel these emotions, it does not mean that your PTSD symptoms are returning. You may be experiencing stress related to other issues like anybody else would. You have worked hard to take control back from PTSD, and you have learned that you can handle your distress. The skills you learned in treatment can help you deal with other distressing situations that happen in your life. What are some ways that you can manage your stress?

Write group members' responses on the board.

Farewells (5 Minutes)

These are typically not final farewells as happen in graduation; rather, they are a chance for everyone to celebrate the group accomplishments.

Day 10

Session 9: Individual Imaginal Exposure (90 Minutes)

Materials Needed

- Devices (PE coach, smartphone, or other digital recording method)
- Binder with Session Handouts (see Appendix A in this guide: Handout 6: Imaginal Exposure Homework Recording Form)
- Handout 5: Therapist Imaginal Exposure Recording Form
- Session Checklist (see Appendix B in this guide)

Session Outline

- Review homework (10 minutes)
- Conduct imaginal exposure (60 minutes) and processing (15 minutes)
- Assign homework (5 minutes)

Review Homework (10 Minutes)

Briefly review imaginal and in vivo homework assignments. Review SUDS and patient experience briefly as in the previous sessions. Address avoidance, provide praise, and problem-solve any issues with completing the homework, as consistent with Foa, Hembree, Rothbaum and Rauch (2019). Work with the PE-IOP team as needed to support and resolve.

Conduct Imaginal Exposure (60 Minutes) and Processing (15 Minutes)

In the final session, consistent with standard PE (Foa, Hembree, Rothbaum, & Rauch, 2019), the therapist goes back to the whole memory exposure for about 60 minutes, and then processing focuses on a review of changes in the patient's ability to approach the memory and reminders, as well as increases in patient competence to manage negative affect and difficult situations. Relapse prevention focuses on a discussion of skills learned and how to apply them if symptoms return. Specifically, the therapists review returning to the skills that worked in treatment to approach instead of avoid trauma memories and reminders. In addition, therapists discuss how, when people are under stress, sometimes they may start to feel emotions that feel a lot like PTSD symptoms. In those times, it is good to pay attention to those emotions and reactions and decide if they are a normal stress reaction to a tough situation or a return of some PTSD symptoms. If they are a reaction to stress, then using the positive coping and normal stress management skills should be effective to manage the stressful time. If they are PTSD symptoms, patients can consider whether they can use their PTSD treatment skills on their own, based on how they have approached instead of avoided in PE-IOP. If they need more help, they can reach out to the PE-IOP team or their local team for a booster session to get them back on track.

Assign Homework (5 Minutes)

▪ Instruct the patient to continue working on additional memory exposures as needed.

Day 10

Session 10: Planned Self-Directed In Vivo Exposure (2 Hours)

Following the plan set up collaboratively with the patient, group therapists, and individual therapist, the patient completes at least one last self-directed in vivo exposure. The patient has 2 hours to complete it, and all logistics to support success (travel to the site of the exposure, etc.) have been set up with case manager assistance if needed.

Graduation (1 Hour)

A final group session celebrating graduation for all those who completed the program occurs for an hour each Friday. During this session, the treatment team (all available) and all the patients gather for graduation. Patients are given a chance to talk about their accomplishments in the program. Team members share accounts of patients' progress as well. In order to protect privacy and confidentiality, providers should not disclose any additional information beyond that from group experiences unless the patient is aware and in agreement. Patients receive a token of completion as a sign of their growth and progress. This can be anything from a certificate to a challenge coin or even a stone or other object of meaning. At EHVP, we distribute personalized certificates signed by the treatment team and program directors and a challenge coin.

CHAPTER 5

Case Management

The Prolonged Exposure-Intensive Outpatient Program (PE-IOP) requires effective case management for optimal function. This role can be assumed by a social work case manager or potentially be distributed to others on the treatment team if necessary. However, the role itself is critical to care coordination at all stages of the program. As mentioned in Chapter 3, case management provides:

1. Care coordination as patients come into and out of PE-IOP,
2. Logistic support for completion of the patient treatment work during IOP (i.e., transportation for in vivo exposures and arranging appointments for specific items needed for exposures), and
3. Aftercare planning focusing on next-step goals of how to maintain gains at home, increase social connection, and value consistent living.

In addition, this role can provide follow-up assessment to ensure maintenance of gains and connection to next steps in the discharge plan. Case managers provide the connective tissue for the treatment team to ensure resources are there for implementation of the treatment plan so that the patient can focus on treatment and carrying out the plan.

Prior to Arrival on Site

Case managers have the most contact with patients prior to their arrival on site. Case managers are responsible for ensuring that all paperwork is completed prior to the intake assessment. Depending on program intake procedures, paperwork may vary but will likely include

- releases of information to allow communication and medical records release for current and past treatment providers and
- completion of self-report forms.

Once determination is made that the patient is appropriate for the program, the case manager contacts the patient to discuss program acceptance, review expectations of behavior, and discuss the logistics of his PE-IOP. This process includes completing (A) Handout 13: Example of Blank PE-IOP Treatment Plan & Admission Review Checklist, based on Handout 12: Example of Completed PE-IOP Treatment Plan & Admission Review Checklist, and (B) completing Handout 15: Example of Blank PE-IOP Goal Sheet, based on Handout 14: Example of Completed PE-IOP Goal Sheet, all of which are found in Appendix A of this guide. For those patients who require travel, the case manager works with the patient care coordinator or similar administrative support to set up travel details. If a program requires the patient to make his own arrangements, the case manager should ensure that they have the details so that they can follow the travel process and know if issues arise. The case manager gets all important information about when patients are coming, when they will travel, where they will stay, and how they will arrive on site based on patient preferences, and the case manager then communicates this information to the patient care coordinator, who will arrange travel and hotel accommodations. The case manager reviews the need for paperwork to request leave from employment, child care plans, and other logistics to ensure that when the patient returns home, things are in order to get back to his life. The case manager ensures that there is a home treatment team prior to the patient arriving on site for the IOP. Finally, the case manager reviews an intake treatment plan (Handout 12: Example of Completed PE-IOP Treatment Plan & Admission Review Checklist) to determine any optional and wellness components that need to be included or scheduled. In the Emory Healthcare Veterans Program (EHVP), this most often includes a discussion of wellness components that patients prefer or do not prefer to add to their schedule, neuropsychological assessment, and/or sleep assessment. The case manager then serves as the point of contact for all logistics as the patient comes to the program.

On Site

Once the patient arrives onsite, the case manager provides a calm and familiar voice to welcome the patient and ensure that the treatment plan remains consistent with his goals and that all logistics for the plan have been put in place (appointments scheduled, medications brought if needed, etc.). The case manager reviews resources in the program and explains to the new participant how to access team members if necessary during PE-IOP. The case manager meets with the patient daily during the program to provide encouragement, discuss any logistics that come up while the patient is on site, such as transportation for in vivo exposures or other appointments, forgotten medications or illness appointments, or setting up new appointments for issues that become apparent during the program. Finally, continuing what was started even before patient arrival on-site, the case manager works to solidify a discharge plan. This plan will be modified based on response during the program. The case manager works to maintain connection with the patient's current treatment team or to find alternate resources if that team is no longer appropriate for the patient's needs. The case manager maintains the discharge plan that is reviewed and approved by the patient and all treatment team members prior to discharge. Discharge plans typically include specific items to address continued support or treatment if warranted for posttraumatic stress disorder (PTSD) or other comorbid disorders as well as new wellness and life goals for maintaining gains from the program (refer to Handout 16: Example of Completed PE-IOP Discharge Plan and Handout 17: Example of Blank PE-IOP Discharge Plan, located in Appendix A).

After discharge, case managers follow-up at periodic intervals to ensure that the patient accessed needed resources and to identify any backsliding early so that booster sessions or phone contacts can help prevent relapse. Case managers doing these follow-up contacts pull in treatment team members as needed. In cases where suicide risk has increased, safety planning, crisis management, and connection with local resources is provided.

Specifics of the case management model used for PE-IOP are flexible as long as the functions noted here are addressed within the treatment team. Throughout patient progress in PE-IOP, the case manager supports implementation of the treatment model and provides logistics and emotional support for patients to fully engage and approach their trauma memory and reminders so that they can get the most out of PE-IOP. If issues arise at home or in the program, the case manager is the key team member to enact alterations in the treatment plan consistent with the team treatment planning decisions. In the treatment team meetings, the case manager provides updates on discharge planning and any issues that may have arisen during PE-IOP.

Case managers serve as a friendly and knowledgeable ear for patients during the IOP. They support the treatment goals but also can be a support to the patient since they are not the therapist. Case managers are the glue keeping together the patient and treatment team. Typically, our patients become very attached to their case managers.

CHAPTER 6   Integrative Interventions

Our aim in the intensive outpatient program (IOP) is to reduce symptoms of posttraumatic stress disorder (PTSD) as well as related symptoms, including depression, anxiety, anger, and substance use, while increasing wellness and general functioning. Given that many of our patients' lives have become very restricted due to avoidance and isolation, we want to expand engagement in their lives by helping to fill the time that used to be occupied by symptomatic behavior with healthy behaviors and activities, so we introduce them to these healthier habits during the IOP. Here, we describe in detail the specifics of how the 2-week Emory Healthcare Veterans Program (EHVP) program incorporates these integrative interventions. The specific components can be considered as options for your program to consider. In Chapter 8, we will cover in more detail how to make decisions regarding what to include or exclude based on the evidence base, consistency in treatment model/message, availability, and cost. Of note, we recommend providing positive coping and wellness options for patients to "try-on" during their PE-IOP so that they can consider multiple new coping strategies in order to find one or two new skills or values that can support the next phase of their lives with greatly reduced or no PTSD.

In the EHVP, patients complete a personal training preassessment, an acupuncture health history questionnaire, and a massage assessment prior to their first appointment. Patients are offered participation in two of the following three options: personal training/gym membership, acupuncture, and massage. Other components are offered to all IOP patients. Some of the components of these interventions are discussed in the upcoming sections.

Family and Relationship Management

Recognizing that PTSD can affect all family members and relationships, our Family Program is structured to help the patient rebuild and strengthen relationships by fostering support related to PTSD. Since our program is focused on military veterans, it includes focus on deployment and military stressors, but similar modifications can be created for civilian patient populations. We use the nationally recognized, evidence-based Families Overcoming Under Stress (FOCUS) model (Lester et al., 2011) to help the patient and her family members share her experiences and learn strategies to increase effective communication, problem-solving, and emotional regulation. Specific content is tailored to the patient's individual needs and strengths. Patients may invite a family member or support person to participate in the resilience training. For the family member's or support person's convenience, this training is offered either face to face or through video conferencing; the support person is not required to attend any session in person. We involve the family via telemedicine rather than in person because we want the patient eating, breathing, and sleeping this treatment without distractions that having a family memebr attend might entail.

Substance Use Education

Patients with a substance use history attend a workshop to explore the connection between substance use and PTSD and how substance use can impact recovery. This workshop allows patients to better understand, more specifically, their alcohol or drug use in terms of low risk versus high risk, identify warning signs of a substance use disorder, and gain strategies for making some changes in their substance use if they desire.

Sleep Education

The objectives of the IOP sleep wellness group seminar are to increase understanding of basic sleep–wake functions and associated behaviors and to help patients implement basic changes in their physical environment and behavioral patterns to improve the overall perceived quality of sleep. This group, comprising two 1-hour group sessions, has been designed to achieve these objectives within a brief period of time and is based on the previous work of other sleep researchers who have found this format to be effective in bringing about positive changes in the sleep experience.

Trauma-Sensitive Yoga

The yoga course focuses on mindful movement, relaxed breathing, and restorative rest. Patients have an opportunity to explore gentle stretches that feel comfortable to them, with an invitation to release thoughts and return to the present moment. Each session includes a period of guided relaxation. No prior yoga experience is needed for this style of yoga, which emphasizes relaxation and stress reduction and can aid in emotional regulation. Yoga is provided three times per week for 1 hour per session at the end of the day.

The yoga instructor and all staff clarify for patients that the core of treatment focuses on the imaginal and in vivo exposures, and yoga is presented to support general wellness and as an option for patients to consider for their long-term stress management and life balance. Our yoga instructors are careful not to touch participants during yoga; it is common practice to offer hands-on adjustment during yoga, but this may be triggering for people with PTSD.

Here is suggested language to introduce patients to yoga:

Hatha Yoga is based on principles and practices that integrate body, mind, and spirit. Our trauma-sensitive yoga classes use mindful breath (pranayama), meditation, and gentle movement and postures (asanas) to help us become more connected and comfortable in our bodies. These practices are intended to help focus and calm the mind, create a safe and strong container, release deep-seated tensions from the body, and create an overall sense of well-being.

Here are some general guidelines to help the patient prepare for class:

- Wear comfortable clothing that she can move in.
- Yoga is generally practiced barefoot, but if she needs to keep socks on, that's fine.
- Try not to eat heavily before class. Practicing yoga on a full stomach may cause cramps or leave participants feeling lethargic.
- Because focus is on breathing, it's advised that participants not chew gum during class as they can swallow it and choke. That said, it is up to each patient to make decisions on what she needs.
- Remind patients to avoid wearing heavy oils or perfumes as others may be sensitive to scents.
- Let patients know that if they have any acute injuries or anything they are concerned about to please inform the teacher.
- Instruct patients to please turn their phones to silent or off.
- Though we try to create a safe environment to practice, keep in mind that bodies hold trauma and patients may experience a trigger while practicing. If this does occur, the instructor should allow the patient to regain balance and return to the present moment.

Finance and Careers

Another area of integrative intervention to consider involves providing resources and support for returning to employment or volunteer service with the aim of finding new meaningful life goals and concrete steps to realizing those goals. This component is brief, but important to ensure that patients leave the program thinking about the next step in their lives rather than only being concerned about where they have been. The EHVP IOP Career and Financial Improvement programming is provided to encourage specific outcome measures in regards to career assessment, career training, career advancement, financial assessment, and financial planning. The session covers topics related to resumé building, financial literacy, and transitioning into a civilian career. Each session identifies defined objectives, and, upon completion of the coursework, participants are equipped with the tools necessary to assist in the successful transition from military to civilian life. This course content was developed for the Department of Defense Yellow Ribbon Reintegration Program by the Clearinghouse for Military Family Readiness at Penn

State University and approved for use by EHVP by the Yellow Ribbon Program. Similar programs for civilian or nonmilitary populations may be available through Goodwill Industries and other providers or developed from the military resources.

Recreational Activities

Having fun is a critical piece of a content life. People suffering with PTSD may not even remember the last time they laughed or enjoyed a day. Being able to approach fun again is important for long-term maintenance of gains and quality of life. In service to this goal, scheduled recreation events are a part of the IOP. Events may include the Georgia Aquarium swim experience, horseback riding, rock climbing, hiking, professional sporting events (e.g., pro baseball, basketball, or football games), and outdoor classes. These events are meant to provide a fun atmosphere as well as an opportunity to learn new skills. While they are designed to be enjoyable, these events are structured also to be consistent with in vivo exposure and behavioral activation, thus getting the patient participating in the outside world with other people.

Addressing Spiritual Issues

For many patients with PTSD, trauma greatly impacted their sense of their own morality and spirituality. Experiencing trauma can be disruptive to our understanding of our spirituality and established belief structure in such a way that makes it difficult to integrate the traumatic experience into our understanding of ourselves, the world, and spirituality. For some patients, this may include a sense that they harmed others and are "bad" because of it, often referred to as *perceived perpetration* or *moral injury*. While many clinical providers and researchers consider this concept within military populations only, having to make difficult choices within the context of trauma can occur with any type of trauma and impact a patient's sense of self and others. The Making Meaning of Service group is facilitated by a pastoral consultant (i.e., chaplain) and gives patients a safe space in which to process and explore how invisible wounds have impacted their beliefs and views about service by exploring questions of meaning, purpose, and values. Patients are able to meet with the pastoral consultant after the group or schedule a time to meet for a one-on-one session to discuss their needs and to foster growth in their beliefs and/or spirituality. Access to such discussions and contact with pastoral resources can be a critical piece of recovery for some patients and is an excellent integrative intervention for PE-IOP. Of note: as with other integrative resources, it is key to ensure that pastoral resources are aware of the program model and rationale to prevent misunderstanding or patients getting different messages across program components.

Wellness Sessions

Establishing new values and life goals often includes considering current health and wellness and setting new goals for how to best take care of oneself for a long, healthy, and happy life. Each patient has an initial wellness review (prior to coming to the program), followed by a planning session once they begin the program. These sessions include motivational interviewing to focus on change and establish specific and achievable goals for IOP as well planning for aftercare. The initial review is then followed by at least one wellness session follow-up and potentially more if the goals warrant additional review. Goals coming out of these sessions may include nutritional changes (such as managing diabetes or other health conditions, general weight loss, or changes to boost general energy), exercise changes, smoking or tobacco use reduction or cessation, and starting meditative or mindfulness practice.

Mindfulness Sessions

While not a required part of PE-IOP, many patients enjoy the opportunity to consider and "try-on" a mindfulness practice. EHVP includes two optional sessions of focused mindfulness practice aimed at providing options for beginning such a practice as well as connection to resources to support continued practice if the patient is interested. Again, this is clearly presented as a way to maintain gains and cope with moving forward in one's life and not as the key element in reducing PTSD.

Personal Training/Gym Membership

Patients in IOP may elect to receive personal training and a 2-week gym membership at a sports center two blocks from their hotel and our treatment facility. For some patients starting or regaining physical fitness practice can bring meaning and a sense of accomplishment to life while also controlling stress and reducing physical health issues.

Resources for Common Comorbidities in PE-IOP Populations

While many of the most common comorbidities are similar across military and civilian PTSD populations, frequency, severity, and type may vary. Program designers are encouraged to consider the inclusion of brief modules to address the most common comorbidities found in their patients, either to assess and plan for aftercare or to determine if such comorbidities can be addressed within the brief IOP format. The following sections provide brief descriptions of the EHVP modules we include.

Chronic Pain Management Group

The Chronic Pain Management group is designed to help patients better understand chronic pain and how it contributes to anxious and depressed mood, substance use, and other difficulties. This group includes two 1-hour sessions where the patient focuses on learning therapeutic skills to manage thoughts, emotions, and behaviors that continue the cycle of chronic pain.

Anger Management Group

The Anger Management group is designed for patients who endorse chronic difficulties with anger and aggression and are interested in learning how to change their behaviors and thoughts to reduce anger in their everyday lives. Many of our patients report anger in addition to other trauma-related and emotional health difficulties. Anger can contribute to these other problems and can lead to major difficulties in social, relational, and occupational functioning. This group includes two 30-minute sessions that help provide skills for anger and aggression management for patients receiving care through the IOP.

Massage Therapy

Whether for pain management, general relaxation, in vivo exposure, or sleep, massage therapy can be a useful strategy for patients to consider while in IOP. Massage therapy involves working on the body with pressure. There are many types of massage, and they may range from light stroking to deep pressure. Swedish massage (also known as "relaxing massage") involves lighter pressure. Deep tissue massage usually involves more pressure as the therapist tries to release tension and "knots" in deeper layers of muscle. Massage has been shown to reduce stress and muscle tension and increase blood circulation in the body. Some studies have shown that those with chronic pain find massage helpful in alleviating pain, increasing mobility, and improving sleep.

Acupuncture

As with massage, acupuncture may be used for chronic pain management, general relaxation, or sleep. Our IOP provides an opportunity for patients to "try-on" acupuncture to determine if this is something they want to use long term for their identified issues.

CHAPTER 7

Daily Session Schedule

The Prolonged Exposure-Intensive Outpatient Program (PE-IOP) involves both group in vivo exposure and individual imaginal exposure sessions (described in Chapter 4), as well as additional treatment components. In this chapter, we present the daily schedules and how we suggest they be used in PE-IOP.

Day 1 (Monday)

- Arrival to Program and Orientation (1 hour)
- Baseline and Additional Assessment (30 minutes; more as necessary)
- Case Management Session (30 minutes)
- Group In Vivo Exposure Session 1 (2 hours)
- Integrative Wellness and Comorbid Issues Intervention (variable)

Arrival to Program and Orientation (1 Hour)

The majority of our patients actually arrive at the hotel on Sunday. In order to begin with clear and shared expectations, PE-IOP begins with a review of rules of behavior and expectations. As noted in Chapter 5 on case management, these rules are not new for the patients because they have already been provided to them in preparation for attendance and have been reviewed with a case manager either in person or by phone. Presenting these together in a group, with each member signing the rules, provides a shared sense of expectations. Orientation allows for people to begin to settle into the new environment and meet group members and staff. Patients need to know that their attendance and participation in all aspects of the program are mandatory. They need to know what happens if they miss sessions or interfere with the progress of other patients in any way. The details of how to handle expectations will be variable based on your practice setting and must balance the needs of the individual patient and the group as well as provide community resources for alternate care if the patient is not able to work within the PE-IOP program. Handout 19 is a sample of the behavioral expectations form and is provided in Appendix A of this guide.

Patients are presented with PE-IOP binders that include all the materials (handouts, etc.) they will need for the duration of the program. They are asked to carry their binders with them to all appointments. The binder also includes brief staff bios and photos. For the Emory Healthcare Veterans Program (EHVP), this orientation session is staffed by Veteran Outreach Coordinators. However, any team member who knows how the program works can provide this orientation.

While some programs may begin with a full first day to include additional exposure, our program allows some flexibility for additional assessment and for travel complications by leaving more unscheduled time and presenting basic psychoeducation as the content on Day 1.

Baseline and Additional Assessment (30 Minutes; More as Needed)

As described in Chapter 3, all patients complete self-report posttraumatic stress disorder (PTSD) and depression measures at program arrival to confirm diagnosis and for use in the assessment of treatment response. This often includes an assessment related to alcohol and drug use and/or medical assessments relevant to medications and physical issues or fitness to engage in other PE-IOP activities (exercise, etc.). If significant time has passed since the intake, Day 1 offers a chance for a reassessment of PTSD symptoms at the start of the program and clarification of the target trauma.

Case Management Session (30 Minutes)

As described in more detail in Chapter 5, the first case management session focuses on travel, the patient PE-IOP Treatment Plan, and the program schedule. The case manager and patient discuss any issues with the plan or changes that may be required. They review resources in the program and how to access team members if necessary during PE-IOP.

Group In Vivo Exposure Session 1 (2 Hours)

Session 1 of group in vivo exposure covers the majority of psychoeducation for exposure therapy in a group format to enhance group cohesion and efficiently present the rationale. Patients begin to create their in vivo exposure hierarchies and lay the foundation to start imaginal exposure in their individual therapy session the next day.

Integrative Wellness and Comorbid Issues Interventions (Variable)

This component of the program provides a place where variance between programs is allowed, but all PE-IOP programs should include some sort of discussion of comorbidities and wellness and integrate some intervention if possible. As previously discussed, the PE-IOP offers the opportunity for patients to consider new goals and life values as their PTSD symptoms are reduced or resolve. Providing clear opportunities for patients to think about what they want to do to maintain gains and feel valued in their lives can help to increase motivation, functioning, and quality of life over time. See Chapter 6 for details.

Day 1 typically involves wellness planning and an assessment of personal goals that may include reengaging with physical exercise, yoga, meditation, nutrition, etc. The case manager has begun the conversation and established the patient's schedule, consistent with what he has requested. In EHVP, the wellness sessions are conducted by a provider who is not the patient's therapist or case manager. This independence is not a requirement.

Day 2 (Tuesday)

- Case Management Session (30 minutes)
- Individual Imaginal Exposure and Processing Session 1 (90 minutes)

- Group In Vivo Exposure Session 2 (2 hours)
- Medical Assessment (1 hour)
- Integrative Wellness and Comorbid Issues Intervention (variable)

Case Management Session (30 Minutes)

Day 2 case management focuses on a review of how the patient is settling in and how Day 1 went. The case manager and patient discuss any issues with the treatment plan or changes that may be required. Discharge planning continues. See Chapter 5.

Individual Imaginal Exposure Session 1 (90 Minutes)

The first imaginal exposure session reviews the rationale presented in the group in vivo session from Day 1 and applies it to imaginal exposure. The patient and therapist then complete the first imaginal exposure and processing.

Group In Vivo Exposure Session 2 (2 Hours)

The second group in vivo exposure focuses on expanding the in vivo hierarchy. The group then completes an in vivo exposure either all together, in small groups, or individually, depending on the hierarchy items.

Medical Assessment (1 Hour)

Medical assessment to review labs, current medications, and physical health occurs early to ensure patients and the PE-IOP team members are aware of medical issues and current status. Any identified issues are added to the treatment plan as appropriate. Given the brevity of the program, we do not typically make changes in medications, but if medications will interfere with progress (such as taking benzodiazepines prior to exposure sessions or practice), we provide the patient with guidance. In addition, recommendations and consultation with current prescribing providers may be warranted for overall discharge planning to maintain gains over time. In EHVP, this medical assessment is provided by a nurse practitioner supervised by a psychiatrist who acts as our medical director.

Integrative Wellness and Comorbid Issues Intervention (Variable)

Day 2 includes a sleep psychoeducation group, yoga, and continued work toward the patient's individual wellness goals with nutrition, massage, acupuncture, or personal training. See Chapter 6 for details.

Day 3 (Wednesday)

- Case Management Session (30–60 minutes)
- Assessment (30 minutes)
- Individual Imaginal Exposure and Processing Session 2 (90 minutes)
- Group In Vivo Exposure Session 3 (2 hours)
- Medication Psychoeducation Group (1 hour)
- Integrative Wellness and Comorbid Issues Intervention (variable)

Case Management Session (30–60 Minutes)

Case management continues to focus on ensuring that logistics are in place for completion of all treatment plan exposures and discharge planning. See Chapter 5.

Assessment (30 Minutes)

Self-report measures of PTSD and depression (and others if indicated) are completed and reviewed with the patient. This review may occur in individual imaginal exposure sessions with therapists or with the case manager.

Individual Imaginal Exposure Session 2 (90 Minutes)

Session 2 of imaginal exposure continues with exposure to the full memory and processing.

Group In Vivo Exposure Session 3 (2 Hours)

Session 3 of group in vivo exposure continues, with group members completing in vivo exposure alone or in groups as appropriate for each participant's hierarchy. In addition, we present a discussion of safety behaviors and address avoidance.

Medication Psychoeducation Group (1 Hour)

A prescribing provider reviews the use of medication for mental health and other common issues in the group. Psychoeducation is tailored to the needs of the group to clarify why members are taking certain medications and how to most effectively take the mediations (i.e., take at the same time each day; medications are only effective if taken each day; some medications control blood sugar and may have an impact at time of administration; the possible impact of medications taken together; and what to take at bedtime vs. morning administration). The goal of the group is to increase patient understanding of medications and the role that medication management can play in reaching treatment and life goals. Many of our patients report being on multiple medications, and they have no idea why they're taking them.

Integrative Wellness and Comorbid Issues Intervention (Variable)

As previously mentioned and provided in more detail in Chapter 6, integrative wellness and comorbid issues interventions vary between programs but should balance the provision of some general coping and community connection resources. For our program, Day 3 includes yoga and connection with community groups as well as continued work toward the patient's individual wellness goals with nutrition, massage, acupuncture, or personal training.

Day 4 (Thursday)

- Case Management Session (30–60 minutes)
- Individual Imaginal Exposure and Processing Session 3 (90 minutes)
- Group In Vivo Exposure Session 4 (2 hours)
- Integrative Wellness and Comorbid Issues Intervention (variable)

Case Management Session (30–60 Minutes)

Case management continues to focus on ensuring that logistics are in place for completion of all treatment plan exposures and discharge planning. See Chapter 5.

Individual Imaginal Exposure and Processing Session 3 (90 Minutes)

Imaginal exposure in Session 3 may move to hot spots–focused exposures and processing if the patient has habituated to the whole memory.

Group In Vivo Exposure Session 4 (2 Hours)

Session 4 of group in vivo exposure continues with group members completing in vivo exposure alone or in groups as appropriate for each participant's hierarchy.

Integrative Wellness and Comorbid Issues Intervention (Variable)

Integrative wellness and comorbid issues interventions vary between programs but should balance the provision of some general coping and community connection resources. For our program, Day 4 includes yoga and finance as well as continued work toward the patient's individual wellness goals with nutrition, massage, acupuncture, or personal training. See Chapter 6 for details.

Day 5 (Friday) and Day 6 (Monday)

- Case Management Session (30 minutes)
- Assessment (30 minutes)
- Individual Imaginal Exposure and Processing Sessions 4 and 5 (90 minutes)
- Group In Vivo Exposure Sessions 5 and 6 (2 hours)
- Integrative Wellness and Comorbid Issues Intervention (variable)

Case Management Session (30 Minutes)

Case management continues to focus on ensuring that logistics are in place for completion of all treatment plan exposures and discharge planning. See Chapter 5.

Assessment (30 Minutes)

Self-report measures of PTSD and depression (and others if indicated) are completed and reviewed with the patient. This review may occur in individual imaginal exposure sessions with therapists or with the case manager.

Individual Imaginal Exposure and Processing Sessions 4 and 5 (90 Minutes)

Sessions 4 and 5 continue with hot spots exposure and processing or move to a second trauma memory if the first memory is processed and processing of a second memory is required.

Group In Vivo Exposure Sessions 5 and 6 (2 Hours)

Sessions 5 and 6 of group in vivo exposure continues, with group members completing in vivo exposure alone or in groups as appropriate for each patient's hierarchy. As members progress up the hierarchy, they are given additional support to plan their own exposures.

Integrative Wellness and Comorbid Issues Intervention (Variable)

Integrative wellness and comorbid issues interventions vary between programs but should balance the provision of some general coping and community connection resources. For our program, Day 5 includes family intervention, mindfulness, and community connection as well as continued work toward the patient's individual wellness goals with nutrition, massage, acupuncture, or personal training. Day 6 includes nutrition and continued work toward the patient's individual wellness goals with nutrition, massage, acupuncture, or personal training. See Chapter 6 for details.

Day 7 (Tuesday)

- Case Management Session (30 minutes)
- Individual Imaginal Exposure and Processing Session 6 (90 minutes)
- Group In Vivo Exposure Session 7 (2 hours)
- Integrative Wellness and Comorbid Issues Intervention (variable)

Case Management Session (30 Minutes)

Case management continues to focus on ensuring that logistics are in place for completion of all treatment plan exposures and discharge planning. See Chapter 5.

Individual Imaginal Exposure and Processing Session 6 (90 Minutes)

Session 6 continues with hot spots exposure and processing, or with a move to a second trauma memory if the first memory is processed and processing of a second memory is required.

Group In Vivo Exposure Session 7 (2 Hours)

Session 7 of group in vivo exposure continues with group members completing in vivo exposure alone or in groups as appropriate for each patient's hierarchy. As members progress up the hierarchy, they are given additional support to plan their own exposures.

Integrative Wellness and Comorbid Issues Intervention (Variable)

Integrative wellness and comorbid issues interventions vary between programs but should balance the provision of some general coping and community connection resources. For our program, Day 7 includes yoga, family intervention, and sleep education as well as continued work toward the patient's individual wellness goals with nutrition, massage, acupuncture, or personal training. See Chapter 6 for details.

Day 8 (Wednesday)

- Case Management Session (30 minutes)
- Assessment (30 minutes)
- Individual Imaginal Exposure and Processing Session 7 (90 minutes)
- Group In Vivo Exposure Session 8 (2 hours)
- Integrative Wellness and Comorbid Issues Intervention (variable)

Case Management Session (30 Minutes)

Case management continues to focus on ensuring that logistics are in place for completion of all treatment plan exposures and discharge planning. See Chapter 5.

Assessment (30 Minutes)

Self-report measures of PTSD and depression (and others if indicated) are completed and reviewed with the patient. This review may occur in individual imaginal exposure sessions with therapists or with the case manager.

Individual Imaginal Exposure and Processing Session 7 (90 Minutes)

Session 7 continues with hot spots exposure and processing, or with a move to a second trauma memory if the first memory is processed and processing of a second memory is required.

Group In Vivo Exposure Session 8 (2 Hours)

Session 8 of group in vivo continues with group members completing in vivo exposure alone or in groups, as appropriate for each patient's hierarchy. Since the next session is the last in vivo group session, group members should have completed most if not all of the items on the hierarchy. If they have not, then a group leader should talk with them individually about their next steps and discuss planning to accomplish those tasks. This can also occur in individual imaginal exposure sessions if more discussion or intervention is needed.

Integrative Wellness and Comorbid Issues Intervention (Variable)

Integrative wellness and comorbid issues interventions vary between programs but should balance the provision of some general coping and community connection resources. For our program, Day 8 includes yoga, family intervention, and community connection as well as continued work toward the patient's individual wellness goals with nutrition, massage, acupuncture, or personal training. See Chapter 6 for details.

Day 9 (Thursday)

- Case Management Session (30 minutes)
- Individual Imaginal Exposure and Processing Session 8 (90 minutes)
- Final Group In Vivo Exposure Session 9 (2 hours)
- Medical Follow-up (30 minutes)
- Integrative Wellness and Comorbid Issues Intervention (variable)

Case Management Session (30 Minutes)

Case management continues to focus on ensuring that logistics are in place for completion of all treatment plan exposures and discharge planning. See Chapter 5.

Individual Imaginal Exposure and Processing Session 8 (90 Minutes)

Session 8 continues with hot spots exposure and processing, or with a move to a second trauma memory if the first memory is processed and processing of a second memory is required.

Final Group In Vivo Exposure Session 9 (2 Hours)

As the final group in vivo session, the group reviews progress on their hierarchies and discusses what is done and what needs more work. In addition, relapse prevention is discussed.

Medical Follow-Up (30 Minutes)

This is the final meeting with the medical team to ensure that the patient's discharge plan is in place. Consultation with providers at home is completed as necessary.

Integrative Wellness and Comorbid Issues Intervention (Variable)

Integrative wellness and comorbid issues interventions vary between programs but should balance the provision of some general coping and community connection resources. For our program, Day 9 includes yoga and family intervention as well as continued work toward the patient's individual wellness goals, planning for after discharge, and how to continue wellness practices.

Day 10 (Friday)

- Case Management Session (30 minutes)
- Final Individual Imaginal Exposure and Processing Session 9 (90 minutes)
- Planned Self-Directed In Vivo Exposure (2 hours)
- Integrative Wellness and Comorbid Issues Intervention (variable)
- Graduation (1 hour)

Case Management Session (30 Minutes)

Case management continues to focus on ensuring that logistics are in place for completion of all treatment plan exposures and discharge planning. See Chapter 5.

Individual Imaginal Exposure and Processing Session 9 (90 Minutes)

The final imaginal exposure and processing session puts the whole memory back together and reviews progress in the program and how participants' thoughts about the self and the world have changed. Finally, discussion of relapse prevention and farewells close the session.

Planned Self-Directed In Vivo Exposure (2 Hours)

Patients complete any final in vivo exposures that were planned in the last session of group in vivo exposure on their own.

Integrative Wellness and Comorbid Issues Intervention (Variable)

Typically, all wellness and comorbid issues sessions have been completed, but if issues arose in scheduling or due to illness, final sessions may occur on the last day.

Graduation (1 Hour)

During the graduation ceremony, both patients and the treatment team share their accomplishments in the program and give farewells. In EHVP, patients receive a certificate signed by their therapist and the program directors, and each participant also receives a challenge coin.

CHAPTER 8

Variations and How to Decide

This therapist guide presents the scaffold and structure for the Prolonged Exposure-Intensive Outpatient Program (PE-IOP). The program is centered on exposure as provided through individual imaginal exposure and group in vivo exposure. The format presented is based primarily on the model used in the Emory Healthcare Veterans Program (EHVP), but this chapter provides a focus on the most common variations in program design along with a discussion of how to decide between the different potential variations.

Program Duration

Massed exposure programs have varied in duration and frequency. We begin here with a discussion of duration. Models with the most research support are 2 or 3 weeks in duration, with at least once-daily individual imaginal exposure. When considering program duration, program designers should consider clinical outcomes and retention and also consider issues of patient presentation, including the patient's ability to stay for the duration of the program. Patients find longer programs are harder to get time away from life responsibilities such as family and work. Programs lasting more than 2 weeks away may be too difficult for working patients who may not want to tell their employers about the reason for their leave. As a result, such programs may only be feasible for more functionally impaired patients. In addition, regardless of the program length, consider the ability to flex program length for those participants who may be slow responders. For instance, in EHVP, if patients have less than a 10-point reduction in their total score on the Posttraumatic Stress Disorder (PTSD) Checklist (the PCL) in Week 1, we consider whether adding a third week or augmenting their second week in PE-IOP is warranted and acceptable to the patient. Specifically, we have been examining augmenting prior to imaginal exposures in the second week of the program with an intervention such as transcranial magnetic stimulation (TMS) or exercise combined with PE.

Exposure Frequency

In addition to duration, programs can vary in the frequency of either individual imaginal exposure or group in vivo exposure. In most cases, this variability is simply one session or two sessions per day plus at least one independent practice. As mentioned in Chapter 2, the specifics of an intensive outpatient PE program used in the studies out of Europe included two exposure sessions (one using the PE method of imaginal exposure and another using the eye movement desensitization and reprocessing model) separated by exercise—a very interesting way to potentially enhance processes involved in learning. Maximizing exposures done with a therapist is typically thought to be a good use of program time. However, the opportunity for patients to have experience with both the therapist-directed exposure and independent exposure work each day can provide opportunities for patients to experience mastery and competence.

Addressing Multiple Traumas

An alternate model presented in the Strong Star research group (Foa et al., 2018) begins with a plan to conduct individual imaginal exposure to the top three target traumas, beginning with the least distressing and working up to the most distressing trauma. The rationale has been that combat PTSD is often the result of multiple traumas, and beginning with the least distressing of the top three traumas will result in patients having less difficulty addressing the worst trauma when they get to it. Data have not been presented to date to support that this works better than other PE models for multiple traumas that start with the most difficult trauma and work down from there (as presented in this guide and the standard PE guide). In the EHVP, while we have seen that many patients have multiple traumas, beginning with the most distressing trauma has been effective and acceptable with patients. In the interest of efficiency and in the absence of data showing higher retention or better outcomes, we would recommend sticking with the standard PE model for addressing multiple traumas, starting with the most distressing trauma that the patient is willing to approach and then, when that is processed, moving on to the next trauma that is connected to PTSD symptoms until they are all processed.

End-of-Day Processing

Another variation for programs to consider is to add a short (15- to 30-minute) processing session with the individual therapist at the end of each day. Such a session allows for a final patient check-in with the individual imaginal exposure therapist to summarize the day and focus the patient on any success achieved in approaching the trauma memory and reminders that day. Such a session would also allow a discussion of any possible negative thoughts about oneself and the world that are maintaining PTSD and alterations that may support therapeutic change.

Rotating Versus Stable Exposure Therapists

Programs can consider models for staffing the individual imaginal exposures and group in vivo exposures with stable staffing or rotating staffing. Stable staffing can allow the patient to establish rapport with the provider, potentially further opening the processing discussion across sessions more fully since there is retention of progress across sessions. Rotating staffing may allow for additional novel insight as new providers bring new perspectives while the patient provides the continuity across sessions. Rotating staffing also has the advantage of more flexibility with staff schedules and absences for work travel, vacation, or illness.

Rationale for Individual Trauma Memory Exposure

One reason for the completion of all trauma memory exposures in individual imaginal exposure sessions is that this allows the program to include people with varied trauma histories in all group elements of PE-IOP. This organization provides efficiency and allows for quick entry into the program over models that require a full cohort of a specific trauma type (such as combat trauma, or military sexual trauma, or civilian sexual assault). Getting patients with PTSD into effective intervention as soon as they decide they want treatment can increase motivation and enhance retention. The adage "strike while the iron is hot" definitely applies to PTSD treatment in that providers need to grab patients the moment they decide treatment is warranted and before the avoidance flows back in and the patient does not follow through.

Breathing Retraining

While the version of PE-IOP presented in this guide does not include breathing retraining, some programs may decide to include this content. It was not included in our standard protocol because the PE-IOP individual sessions start with imaginal exposure for maximum efficiency. To maximize efficiency and retain individual session time for imaginal exposure, we suggest that if breathing retraining is being added to the PE-IOP program, the content may be added to other psychoeducation provided in Session 1, in a group setting with practice to follow.

Some patients find this technique extremely useful and use it while others do not. We instruct patients not to use breathing retraining during exposure exercises because we want them to experience their ability to cope with trauma-related memories and situations without special devices. In our view, the breathing skill is not critical to the process and outcome of PE. If breathing retraining is being used in your program, for Session 1 homework, instruct the patient to read Handout 1: Rationale for Treatment by Prolonged Exposure, listen to the session recording one time before the next session, and practice the breathing retraining on a daily basis. Handout 18: Breathing Retraining Technique will facilitate the practice of this exercise.

The rationale for this technique is as follows:

> *Very often, when people become frightened or upset, they feel like they need more air and may therefore breathe fast or hyperventilate.*

Hyperventilation, however, does not have a calming effect. In fact, it generates anxious feelings. Unless we are preparing for fighting or fleeing from real danger, we often don't need as much air as we are taking in. When we hyperventilate and take in more air, it signals our bodies to prepare for fighting or fleeing and keeps it fueled with oxygen. This is similar to a runner taking deep breaths to fuel the body with oxygen before a race and continuing to breathe deeply and quickly throughout the race. Hyperventilating also produces bodily reactions that resemble fear. These bodily reactions, in turn, can make us more afraid. Usually, though, when we hyperventilate, we are tricking our bodies. And what we really need to do is to slow down our breathing and take in less air. So learning to breathe slowly and calmly provides a useful tool for reducing stress or tension.

*Most of us realize that our breathing also affects the way that we feel. For example, when we are upset, people may tell us to take a deep breath and calm down. We think that it is not really **deep** breathing that helps, but **slow** breathing. In order to calm down or relax, take normal breaths and exhale slowly. It is exhalation (not inhalation) that is associated with relaxation. Also, it can be helpful to associate your exhalation with a word that has a calming or relaxing effect. So while you exhale, say the words "calm" or "relax" silently to yourself very slowly. Like this: c-a-a-a-a-a-l-m.*

When suggesting a cue word for relaxation, the words "calm" or "relax" are most commonly used. Model for the group how to inhale and exhale slowly through the nose and then ask them to perform the exercise according to the following instructions:

In addition to concentrating on slow exhalation while saying "calm" to yourself, I want you to do one other thing to slow down your breathing. After you finish exhaling, and when your lungs are empty of air, I'd like you to pause for a count of 3 or 4 before inhaling again. So it will go like this: "Inhale (a normal breath . . . exhale (very slowly) . . . Caaaaaaaaallllllmmmmm . . . hold 1 . . . 2 . . . 3 . . . 4 . . . Inhale (normal breath) . . . exhale," etc. I will gradually fade away my instructions, but I'd like you to continue with this breathing technique.

After practicing for a few respiratory cycles, repeat the entire breathing sequence 10–15 times: *"Inhale . . . exhale . . . Caaaaaallllmmm . . . hold 1 . . . 2 . . . 3 . . . 4 . . . inhale . . . exhale . . . Caaaaaallllmmm,"* etc. Thus while the group is exhaling slowly, you will say the word "calm" aloud, dragging it out very slowly, to a count of 4. Based on program preferences, patients may then be directed to the PE Coach app or be provided with a recording the program has created to practice between sessions. They are also provided with Handout 18: Breathing Retraining Technique, to practice between sessions.

Alternate Primary Diagnosis

In addition to PE-IOP, the current structure can also support use of the uniform protocol for non-PTSD primary diagnostic issues. For programs that want to consider this, the individual sessions can follow the content of the Unified Protocol for Transdiagnostic Treatment of Emotional Disorders (Barlow & Farchione, 2018) for patients who may not have PTSD but do meet criteria for depression or another anxiety disorder. The group in vivo exposures can then focus on the targeted exposures relevant to the presenting primary diagnosis (interoceptive exposure for panic disorder, etc.). Full details of how to implement these variations are beyond the current therapist guide.

Integrative Components

Many options for positive coping, wellness, and addressing comorbidities were presented in Chapter 6. In deciding what to add to the core of PE-IOP, program designers need to consider three factors:

1. evidence base for identified target,
2. consistency with the message of PE-IOP, and
3. cost/feasibility.

First, the evidence base for the identified target refers to an examination of the literature to determine whether there are studies to support the use of the intervention to complement the core PTSD treatment. The best evidence would be in studies adding the intervention to PE or similar exposure-based protocols, but, barring that, consider studies showing that the intervention added to other effective PTSD interventions can provide useful direction. For instance, yoga and acupuncture have some promising evidence that adding them to other psychotherapy for PTSD may provide benefit.

Next, program designers should examine whether the underlying message of the considered wellness intervention is consistent with the message of PE-IOP. Simply put, the message of PE-IOP is to approach the trauma memory and reminders and stay with the emotions it brings. It gets easier if the patient stays with the memory, and they can come to think of themselves and the memory in a way that is more helpful.

Finally, the program should consider cost and feasibility. With regard to cost, the program should focus on whether the integrative intervention under consideration is at a price point that is sustainable and that provides enough benefit to warrant the expense. With regard to feasibility, the program should consider the time required to get to the intervention and complete procedures required as well as the "opportunity cost." In this context, *opportunity cost* refers to the tradeoff that occurs if the patient is engaging in the integrative interventions; that is, time not available to do exposure or homework. With this in mind, it is best to focus integrative interventions on treatments that can be implemented over time and even back home to maintain positive coping and gains the patient made in the program.

Program Additions: The Bottom Line

In the end, the PE-IOP model should provide an efficient dose of exposure to drive PTSD symptom reduction while at the same time providing options for positive coping and addressing comorbidities that are consistent with the message of PE. The goal of these additions is not necessarily to add to the reduction in PTSD symptoms but rather to increase motivation, enhance general well-being, increase effective stress management, reduce comorbid issues, and improve family, work, or general function. Program designers should be especially cautious to ensure that all providers consistently support that the core change of PE-IOP is driven by the PE, with the other pieces supporting and maintaining that change. All providers must be aware of how PE works and how patients may at times be challenged to engage in difficult exposures so that when patients comment on their treatment, providers can offer appropriate and supportive comments that are consistent with the treatment plan and patient progress. In addition, all team members can discuss any issues that arise in team consultation sessions, as previously described.

Therapist and Patient Handouts

List of Handouts

Day 1

Group In Vivo Exposure Session 1

Handout 1
Rationale for Treatment by Prolonged Exposure

The treatment program you are participating in is called Prolonged Exposure. Exposure in this sense means facing thoughts, feelings, or situations that you might have been avoiding because they trigger distress.[1] There are two main parts to this program.

The first is *imaginal exposure,* in which you revisit the trauma memory repeatedly in your mind. In this intensive outpatient program (IOP), you will practice imaginal exposure in daily individual sessions with your therapist. The second part is in vivo *exposure,* in which you confront safe or low-risk situations that you have been avoiding after your trauma. In this IOP, you will engage in in vivo *exposure,* typically in a group with the other patients and a group leader. Many people who have experienced a trauma try to avoid thoughts and feelings associated with that event. Similarly, many people avoid situations, places, and activities that remind them of the trauma or that just feel scary. However, while avoiding can make you feel more comfortable in the short run, it actually can make the problem worse in the long run because it prevents you from overcoming your fears. Imaginal and in vivo exposure address these problems and work in similar ways.

How does exposure work? When you confront feared memories or situations in a systematic way under relatively safe circumstances, several things happen:

1. Revisiting the memory helps to emotionally process the traumatic experience and make sense of it.

2. You learn that thinking about a traumatic experience is not dangerous and that being upset or anxious is not dangerous.

3. You become less fearful of other situations that remind you of your trauma.

4. You learn that you can handle your distress, and you feel better about yourself.

5. Finally, you learn that when you repeatedly confront memories or situations you have avoided, the fear and distress gradually decrease. In other words, you again become relatively comfortable in these situations. We call this *habituation,* which is the process by which anxiety comes down on its own. When you stick it out and stay in a frightening but safe situation for a long enough time and you go

---

[1] This material originally was published as Handout 1 in *Reclaiming Your Life from a Traumatic Experience WORKBOOK* (2nd ed.) (Rothbaum et al., 2019). Reprinted by permission of Oxford University Press.

back to that same situation often enough, you simply become less frightened of this situation. In a way, it is similar to getting back on a bicycle after falling off. If you refuse to try again, over time you become more and more frightened of riding bicycles. But if you get back on and ride your bicycle despite your fear, you become less and less afraid.

Habituation works with frightening memories, too. Letting yourself engage in the traumatic memories rather than avoiding them will allow you to remember the trauma with less distress, and you will learn that the memories are not dangerous. Exposure to the painful memories (i.e., revisiting the trauma in imagination) allows you to gain control over them so they will be less likely to pop up at times you do not want them to. The flashbacks, nightmares, and intrusive thoughts that many trauma survivors often experience are less likely to occur after you repeatedly revisit the trauma memories, and, when they do occur, they are less upsetting.

Following a trauma, people's beliefs about themselves and about the world may change in basic ways. You may view situations as dangerous when, before the trauma, such situations would not have bothered you at all. You may find that your attitude toward people and the world in general has become more negative than it used to be or that your self-image has gotten worse. Many times these changes reflect trauma-related changes in your thinking. Sometimes even the presence of posttraumatic stress disorder (PTSD) may cause you to think and feel negatively about yourself. Because how you think about yourself, the world, and other people affects how you feel, it is useful to pay attention to how the traumatic experience has shaped your thoughts and beliefs. For this reason, as you go through the treatment, you and your therapist will discuss how you think about the trauma, yourself, other people, and situations in your life. You will sometimes explore trauma-related changes in your thinking and see how such changes affect your feelings and whether they are helpful or not.

Treatment by imaginal and in vivo exposure may seem difficult at first, and many trauma survivors are afraid of becoming involved in it. But, with time, you will find that this treatment is challenging and makes you feel good about yourself. Congratulations! You have made the very scary first step in taking back control of your life! You will be glad you did!

Handout 2
Subjective Units of Distress & In Vivo Exposure Hierarchy

Name_____   Date _____

Subjective Units of Distress Scale

Anchors

_____0 = no distress/negative affect/totally relaxed

_____25 = not quite relaxed but not distressed

_____50 = beginning to feel negative affect/distress but it is manageable

_____75 = noticeable distress/negative affect with physiological signs

_____100 = most distress/negative affect ever experienced in your life

List of activities	SUDS rating	SUDS rating
	Beginning of Treatment	End of Treatment

A traumatic experience is an emotional shock and may cause many emotional problems.[2] This section describes some of the common reactions people have after a trauma. Because everyone responds differently to traumatic events, you may have some of these reactions more than others, and some you may not have at all.

Remember, many changes after a trauma are normal. In fact, most people who directly experience a major trauma have severe reactions in the immediate aftermath similar to yours. Many people then feel much better within 3 months after the event, but others recover more slowly, and some do not recover enough without help. Becoming more aware of the changes you have undergone since your trauma is the first step toward recovery.

Some of the most common problems after a trauma are described here.

Negative emotions. One of the primary reactions that people experience after a trauma are *frequent negative emotions* including fear and anxiety, guilt, shame, or anger. Anxiety is a common and natural response to a dangerous situation. For many people, it lasts long after the trauma has ended. This happens when our views of the world and sense of safety have changed and become more negative. You may become anxious when you remember the trauma. In some people, guilt or shame may be the prominent emotions when they have had traumas in which they experienced or witnessed events that felt wrong, immoral, or personally violating. Feelings of anger may also be triggered by traumatic experiences that felt unjust or violating.

These upsetting thoughts and feelings are sometimes triggered by external events, but sometimes they seem to come on by themselves or out of the blue. **Triggers or cues** that can cause distress may include places, times of day, certain smells or noises, or any situation that reminds you of the trauma. As you begin to pay more attention to these times, you can discover the triggers for your distress. In this way, you may learn that some of your out-of-the-blue negative feelings are really triggered by things that remind you of your trauma.

Reexperiencing the trauma. People who have been traumatized often reexperience the traumatic event. For example, you may have **unwanted thoughts** of the trauma and find yourself unable to get rid of them. Some people have **flashbacks**, or very vivid images, as if the trauma is

---

[2] This material originally was published as Handout 3 in *Reclaiming Your Life from a Traumatic Experience WORKBOOK* (2nd ed.) (Rothbaum et al., 2019). Reprinted by permission of Oxford University Press.

occurring again. **Nightmares** are also common. These symptoms occur because a traumatic experience is so shocking and so different from everyday experiences that you can't fit it into what you know about the world. So, in order to understand what happened, your mind keeps bringing the memory back, as if to better digest it and fit it in.

Increased arousal. Another common response to trauma is increased arousal, which includes feeling jumpy, jittery, and shaky; being easily startled; having trouble concentrating; and having trouble sleeping. This is another common experience that results from a trauma. Continuous arousal can lead to **impatience** and **irritability**, especially if you're not getting enough sleep. The arousal reactions are due to the fight-or-flight response in your body. The fight-or-flight response is how we protect ourselves against danger, and it also occurs in animals. When we protect ourselves from danger by fighting or running away, we need a lot more energy than usual, so our bodies pump out extra adrenaline to help us get the extra energy we need to survive.

People who have been traumatized often see the world as filled with danger, so their bodies are on constant alert, always ready to respond immediately to any attack. The problem is that increased arousal is useful in truly dangerous situations, such as if we find ourselves facing a tiger. But alertness becomes very uncomfortable when it continues for a long time even in safe situations. Another reaction to danger is to **freeze**, like a deer in the headlights, and this reaction can also occur during a trauma.

Avoidance. As has been discussed in the patient workbook, avoidance is a common way of managing trauma-related pain and distress. It is a strategy to protect yourself from situations you feel have become dangerous and from thoughts and feelings that are painful, overwhelming, or distressing. You may be avoiding situations that remind you of the trauma, such as activities or people that are related to the traumatic events. Often situations that are less directly related to the trauma are also avoided, such as going out after dark or being in crowded places. Another way to reduce discomfort is to try to push away painful thoughts and feelings. This can lead to feelings of **numbness**, where you find it difficult to have both fearful and pleasant or loving feelings. Some people feel that they have lost their ability to experience positive emotions like happiness, joy, or loving feelings. Sometimes the painful thoughts or feelings may be so intense that your mind just blocks them out altogether, and you may not remember parts of the trauma.

Anger and irritability. Many people who have been traumatized feel angry and irritable. It may be especially confusing to feel angry at those who are closest to you. Sometimes people feel angry because of feeling irritable so often. Anger can also arise from a feeling that the world is not fair.

Guilt and shame. People often experience changes in their thoughts and beliefs after a trauma. They may see the world as a very dangerous place or themselves as weak or bad. Trauma often leads to feelings of guilt and shame. Many people blame themselves for things they did or didn't do. For example, some assault survivors believe that they should have fought off an assailant, and they blame themselves for the assault. Others feel that if they had not fought back they wouldn't have gotten hurt. A veteran may feel guilty for hitting an IED while he was driving that injured or killed a buddy. You may feel ashamed because during the trauma you acted in ways that you would not otherwise have done. Sometimes, other people may blame you for the trauma.

Feeling guilty about the trauma means that you are taking responsibility for what occurred. While this may make you feel somewhat more in control, it can also lead to feelings of helplessness and depression.

Grief and depression. Other common reactions to trauma include grief and depression, such as feeling down, sad, hopeless, or despairing. You may cry more often. Trauma survivors often feel a sense of grief for what they have lost or for who they were before the trauma occurred. Sometimes grieving is associated with the loss of the ability to control what has happened to you or to your body or the loss of your sense of safety. You may lose interest in people and activities you used to enjoy. You may feel that plans you had for the future don't seem to matter anymore, or that life isn't worth living. These feelings can lead to thoughts of wishing you were dead or doing something to hurt or try to kill yourself. Because the trauma has changed so much of how you see the world and yourself, it makes sense to feel sad and to grieve for what you lost because of the trauma.

Self-image and views of other people. How you see yourself and others often becomes more negative after a trauma. You may tell yourself, "If I hadn't been so weak or stupid, this wouldn't have happened to me." Many people see themselves as more negative overall after the trauma ("I am a bad person and deserved this" or "other people experience the same trauma but they remain strong and go on in life").

It is very common to see others more negatively and to feel that you can't **trust** anyone. If you used to think about the world as a safe place, the trauma may suddenly make you think that the world is very dangerous. If you had previous bad experiences, the trauma may convince you that the world is dangerous and others aren't to be trusted. These negative thoughts often make people feel that they have been changed completely and permanently by the trauma. Relationships with others can become tense, and it may be difficult to become intimate with people as your trust decreases.

People sometimes begin to behave in a reckless or self-destructive manner after a trauma. This may include driving too fast, making poor decisions, taking excessive risks. Have you been engaging in reckless or risky behavior? Are friends or family worried about you?

It is not unusual to have disruptions in relationships with other people after a traumatic experience or to struggle with trusting and feeling close with others. Sexual relationships may suffer after a traumatic experience. Many people find it difficult to feel sexual or have sexual relationships. This is especially true for those who have been sexually assaulted since, in addition to the lack of trust, sex itself is a reminder of the assault.

Use of alcohol or drugs. Some people increase their use of alcohol or drugs after a trauma. There is nothing wrong with responsible drinking, but if your use of alcohol or drugs has increased as a result of your traumatic experience, it can slow down your recovery and cause problems of its own.

Interconnections. Many of the reactions to trauma are connected to one another. For example, a flashback may make you feel out of control and will therefore produce fear and arousal. Many people think that their common reactions to the trauma mean that they are "going crazy" or "losing it." These thoughts can make them even more fearful. Again, as you become aware of the changes you have gone through since the trauma and as you process these experiences during treatment, the symptoms should become less distressing.

Handout 4
List of Things to Take Back

Directions: Make a personalized list of the situations, people, places, and things that you avoid and which you want to take back from PTSD.

_____

_____

_____

_____

_____

_____

_____

_____

_____

Example of a List of Things to Take Back

Directions: Make a personalized list of the situations, people, places, and things that you avoid and which you want to take back from PTSD. A list might include some of these example items:

Being able to sit in a restaurant in any seat

Going to the movies

Going out alone

Going out after dark

Dating

Having sex

Going to the grocery store

Standing in line without looking over shoulder

Taking children/grandchildren to the park or playground

Going to worship service

Specific smell that reminds you of traumatic event (for example: diesel, sweat)

Specific sound that reminds you of traumatic event (for example: certain songs, helicopters, gunfire, sirens)

Driving

Traffic

People sitting behind you

Day 2

Individual Imaginal Exposure Session 1

Handout 5
Therapist Imaginal Exposure Recording Form

(for Therapist's Use in Imaginal Exposure)

Name of Client[3]: _____   Therapist: _____

Date: _____   Exposure #: _____   Session #: _____

Description of exposure in imagination: _____

_____

Start time	SUDS	Notes
Beginning	_____	_____
5 minutes	_____	_____
10 minutes	_____	_____
15 minutes	_____	_____
20 minutes	_____	_____
25 minutes	_____	_____
30 minutes	_____	_____
35 minutes	_____	_____
40 minutes	_____	_____
45 minutes	_____	_____
50 minutes	_____	_____
55 minutes	_____	_____
60 minutes	_____	_____

[3] This material originally was published as Handout A in *Prolonged Exposure Therapy for PTSD: Emotional Processing of Traumatic Experiences THERAPIST GUIDE* (2nd ed.) (Foa et al., 2019). Reprinted by permission of Oxford University Press.

Handout 6
Imaginal Exposure Homework Recording Form

Subjective Units of Distress Scale

0 = no distress/negative affect/totally relaxed

25 = not quite relaxed but not distressed

50 = beginning to feel negative affect/distress but it is manageable

75 = noticeable distress/negative affect with physiological signs

100 = the most distress/negative affect you have ever experienced in your life

Date	Length	Pre	Post	Peak	Date	Length	Pre	Post	Peak

Imaginal Exposure Tips

1. **DO NOT** do this exercise right before you want to go to sleep.

2. Find a place where you feel comfortable and remember to **CLOSE YOUR EYES** while you listen to the recording.

3. **STAY WITH YOUR ANXIETY** throughout the exercise. Do not try to reduce it, and do not stop in the middle of the exposure.

4. Allow yourself to **REVISIT AND FEEL** what you thought, emotions you felt, and things you did at the time of the trauma while you are listening to the recording.

5. **DO NOT AVOID** letting yourself experience the memory.

6. Listen to the entire recording all at one time **EVERYDAY**.

7. If you feel overwhelmed or have questions while listening to the recording, call your individual therapist _____ to talk about your exercise.

Day 2

Group In Vivo Exposure Session 2

In vivo exercise: Going to coffee shop

Remember, you can take steps to reach the goal. Each time spent in the coffee shop is 30 to 45 minutes or until SUDS goes down by half.

				Going to coffee shop alone and driving self to and from shop
			Going to coffee shop alone with friend dropping off and picking up	Goal
		Going to coffee shop alone while friend is out in parking lot		
	Going to coffee shop with a friend sitting more in middle of shop			
Going to coffee shop with a friend sitting in back of shop				
Start				

Date:

In vivo exercise:

				Goal
Start				

Handout 8
In Vivo Exposure Homework Recording Form

Name[4]: _____ Date: _____

1. Situation that you practiced _____

Date & Time	SUDS			Date & Time	SUDS		
	Pre	Post	Peak		Pre	Post	Peak
1.				5.			
2.				6.			
3.				7.			
4.				8.			

2. Situation that you practiced _____

Date & Time	SUDS			Date & Time	SUDS		
	Pre	Post	Peak		Pre	Post	Peak
1.				5.			
2.				6.			
3.				7.			
4.				8.			

[4] This material originally was published as Handout 5 in *Reclaiming Your Life from a Traumatic Experience WORKBOOK* (2nd ed.) (Rothbaum et al., 2019). Reprinted by permission of Oxford University Press.

3. Situation that you practiced _____

Date & Time	SUDS			Date & Time	SUDS		
	Pre	Post	Peak		Pre	Post	Peak
1.				5.			
2.				6.			
3.				7.			
4.				8.			

Day 3

Group In Vivo Exposure Session 3

Handout 9
Safety Behaviors

What Are Safety Behaviors?

Safety behaviors are:

- Things that people do or say to temporarily reduce negative feelings that come up in situations.
- They do not actually increase safety, they just make the person feel better temporarily.
- They are not actually related to long-term reductions in anxiety.
- They can result in having to do something more and more often, such as check window locks or carry a medication bottle.
- They are often used by someone with PTSD to reduce the sense of vulnerability to threat in a non-threatening environment (e.g., crowded store).
- They make sense in the short term, but in the long run they maintain negative emotions and prevent you from learning that you can handle the situation and nothing bad happens without the safety behavior.

Why Do People with PTSD Develop Safety Behaviors?

People develop safety behaviors in an attempt to control their emotions in distressing situations. So, just like avoidance, safety behaviors make sense in the short term but take away your control in the long run.

Common types of safety behaviors include:

- Scanning the environment for threat to make sure that there is no danger or a "suspicious" person around
- Checking for exits and points of escape (e.g., at stores or restaurants)
- Carrying a weapon
- Sitting/standing with your back to the wall or in a corner position
- "Casing" a location (e.g., store parking lot) prior to going there to do something you need to do (e.g., shopping)
- "Pulling guard duty" in public locations

Do these look familiar? Can you think of others that you do?

How Do Safety Behaviors Maintain Your PTSD?

■ The problem with safety behaviors is that every time you engage in a safety behavior, your brain concludes that you only escaped the situation without injury because of this safety behavior rather than learning that you can handle the situation on your own or that the situation itself is safe.

■ Safety behaviors reinforce the idea that a relatively safe situation, activity, or person is dangerous unless you do this specific thing. As a result, you often feel that you have to do the safety behavior more and more because the sense of threat never really disappears. This is how hypervigilance often works in PTSD. If you scan once, you feel a little better for a couple minutes, but then you have to scan again and again and again. Pretty soon, you are only scanning and cannot engage in your life.

What Happens If You Stop Engaging in Safety Behaviors in Situations Where You Feel Distressed?

■ When people with PTSD stop engaging in safety behaviors they usually will feel more distressed at first because they have given up something that provides them a brief sense of security. However, with regular practice of in vivo exposure exercises, people learn that they do not need safety behaviors to be safe because the situation is already safe. The result is that you take back control over your life and can go into these situations without being distressed. You may even find that you start to enjoy these activities again because you are no longer excessively focused on threat.

■ People with PTSD are often motivated to do in vivo exposure therapy and stop using safety behaviors in order to reap the long-term benefits associated with these techniques (e.g., being able to enjoy dinner out with your family, being able to shop comfortably at a store, or feeling close to important others).

What are some of the personal benefits that you can think of that might result for you from doing in vivo exposure therapy/giving up safety behaviors?

_____

_____

_____

_____

_____

_____

Day 9

Group In Vivo Exposure Session 9

Handout 10
Relapse Prevention Skills

Remember that when you *confront* rather than *avoid* the activities, places, people, or things that cause distress or anxiety you learn that:

- You can handle being in these situations, places, or interacting with people.
- The negative feelings (such as anxiety or distress) will not last forever.
- These situations are safe.
- You can feel relaxed and don't always have to be on guard.
- You can take back control from anxiety and make your own choices about how you live your life.

Remember the work that you did with your recording and revisiting the memory was to help you:

- Learn that you can handle the memory and the feelings that come with the memory
- Learn that the memory cannot harm you and is not happening now
- Learn that you can think about the memory when you choose, and it does not have control over you
- Remember that if you confront the memory the negative feelings will not last forever

So if you are feeling the urge to avoid places, situations, people, or thoughts and memories—*Think about it.* That may be a sign that you need to *confront not avoid*.

What things might you be avoiding right now that you need to confront?

_____

_____

_____

_____

How can you confront these situations, thoughts, or activities in the future?

_____

_____

_____

_____

Handout 11
Managing Stress

Remember, stress is a normal part of life. You will experience distress, sadness, stress, anxiety, and many other negative emotions in response to things that happen in your life. When you feel these emotions, it does not mean that your PTSD symptoms are returning. You have worked hard to take back control from PTSD, and you have learned that you can handle your distress. The skills you learned in treatment can help you deal with other distressing situations that happen in your life. When you avoid situations or feelings, you are giving those things or feelings more power.

How do you think you can manage some of the stress that is happening in your life now or that might occur in the future?

_____

_____

_____

_____

_____

Examples of ways to manage your everyday stress are listed here:

- Slow breathing
- Meditation
- Good self-care (diet and exercise, healthy sleep habits)
- List of costs and benefits to help with difficult decisions
- Prioritize your responsibilities
- Don't take on too much at once—pace yourself
- Take a time out to gain perspective—come back to the problem when you feel able to be proactive or when you have a strategy
- Schedule leisure time
- Talk to people you trust for advice and support
- Engage in activities that give you a sense of purpose (volunteer, hobbies, clubs, etc.)
- Positive coping statements—Write them on index cards or put them in your phone so you can keep them with you

- Set good boundaries with yourself and others—be assertive
- Use grounding techniques—focus on your senses (visual, touch, etc.) to bring you back to the present moment
- Communicate your needs to others calmly but assertively (e.g., "I'm overwhelmed right now, and it would help if you give me some space to calm down.")

Case Management Forms

Handout 12

Example of Completed PE- IOP Treatment Plan & Admission Review Checklist

(Modify for program specifics)[5]

Patient Information

Name:	John Doe		Date	10/01/2019
IOP Start Date:	10/21/19			

Chart Review (before calling patient)

Phone Number:	xxx	Email	xxx	
Address:	xxx		Local Waitlist? ☐ YES ☒ NO	
MRN:	xxx	Last 4:	xxxx	

Psychiatric Diagnosis:	☒ PTSD ☒ MDD ☐ Bipolar I or II ☐ GAD ☐ OCD ☐ Social Anxiety ☐ Alcohol Use ☐ Drug use ☐ TBI ☐ PDD ☐ PD ☐ Other_____
Medical Diagnosis:	None
Alcohol/ Substance:	None of note
Suicidal Ideation:	Provided Patient's Crisis Line: 1-800-273-8255 Press 1 ☒ YES ☐ NO Weapon? ☐ YES ☒ NO Gun Lock Provided ☐ YES ☒ NO Safety Plan ☐ YES ☒ NO Date:

---

[5] This Handout was created by Lindy Carbone, LCSW, and Megan Goodlin, LCSW. Used with permission.

Treatment Plan from Case Conference:

(From multidisciplinary case conference)

track: _____	Other Recommendations/Notes:

SUD Consult	Healthy Behaviors	UDS	<u>UDS needed?</u>
☐ YES	☐ YES	☐ YES	☐ Pre 9/11
☒ NO	☒ NO	☒ NO	Flying ~ 2 weeks prior

Sleep Consult	Sleep Study	TRD	Driving ~ 1 week prior
☐ YES	☐ YES	☐ YES	**Date for UDS:**
☒ NO	☒ NO	☒ NO	

Acupuncture	Massage
☐ Yes ☐ No	☐ Yes ☒ No
	☐ M ☐ F ☐ Either

Pers. Training	Ind. Pastor Session
☒ Yes ☐ No	☒ Yes ☐ No

Anger Management	☐ YES	☒ NO
Chronic Pain Group	☐ YES	☒ NO
Neuropsych testing	☐ YES	☒ NO
Smoking Cessation	☒ YES	☐ NO
Research	☒ YES	☐ NO

Home Treatment team needed?	Current therapist:	**DD214 received?**
☐ YES ☒ NO	Current PCP/ Psychiatrist: Dr. Jyn	☒ YES ☐ NO

Program Checklist (Call Patient)

How would you like to be addressed while attending the program (e.g., first name, last name?) John or Mr. Doe

Work/School Excuse Letter

Do you need any medical documentation for work or school for you to attend the IOP?

☐ YES ☒ NO

Medication

Do you take medications?

☒ YES   ☐ NO

If you take any medications, please be sure to bring all of your medications for the full 2 weeks.

☒ YES   ☐ NO

Physical Health

Do you have any chronic health issues (for example, diabetes or sleep apnea), physical limitations, or mobility concerns (for example, do you use a cane, walker, or wheelchair)?

☐ YES   ☒ NO

If YES, What are those issues or concerns and plan to address those concerns?

Service Dog

Do you have a service animal? ☐ YES   ☒ NO

Review service animal and relevant program requirements

Legal Needs

Do you have any ongoing legal issues that you would have to attend to while you are in our program (for example, family court, traffic court, or recent arrests)?

☐ YES   ☒ NO

If yes, what are those issues?

Personal Needs

Do you have any housing or other immediate needs that need to be addressed before coming to IOP?

☐ YES   ☒ NO

If yes, what are those issues?

Dietary

Dietary restrictions or food allergies?

☐ YES   ☒ NO

Note Allergy Details:

Determine Patient Communication Needs

Do you have a smartphone or tablet with reliable access to internet? ☒ YES ☐ NO

Explain:

If yes, we will need you to be sure to bring it with you because there are apps that we have you download for the program. If no, then we will provide a recorder for individual sessions.

Rules/Guidelines for IOP

Participation in the IOP is subject to the observance of the organization's rules and procedures. The activities that I am about to outline are strictly prohibited. Any patient who violates this Code is subject to removal from the program.

- *No abusive, rude, and/or disrespectful language toward a staff member, volunteer, or another patient.*
- *Do not use or bring drugs or alcohol to the program, including during travel to and from the program. We do random breathalyzer and drug screens, and a positive result will result in a discussion with your treatment team and could also result in you being sent home early.*
- *Do not bring dangerous or unauthorized materials such as explosives, firearms, or other weapons.*
- *No sexual contact with another patient and no sexual or gender-based harassment of a fellow patient, staff member, or volunteer will be tolerated.*
- *Actual or threatened violence or harm toward yourself, any other individual, or group members will not be tolerated.*

Do you agree to follow these rules and guidelines?
☒ YES ☐ NO
Do you have any questions?
☒ YES ☐ NO

Review Treatment Plan with Patient
Required:

☒ **Wellness Program:** Sleep education, mindfulness, meeting with an individual wellness provider, and trauma-focused gentle yoga	☒ **Finance and Careers:** A class to learn about career and financial opportunities ☒ **Weekend Activity:** Explain that there is a weekend activity on either Saturday or Sunday

Family Therapy

This is a family skills group that provides psychoeducation about PTSD as well as skills to foster resilience.

Would you like a family member to be involved in these sessions via telehealth?

☒ YES ☐ NO

If NO, explain that patient can still participate in family sessions as an individual.

If YES, the family member is a: ☒ Spouse/Partner ☐ Parent ☐ Adult Child ☐ Other
Name and contact number of the Family Member:

Lodging: Program Hotel

Transportation:
Is the patient flying or driving? ☒ Needs Flight ☐ Driving

Flying:
Flight lands 10/20/19 6P; Roger will pick-up and deliver to the hotel

Driving:

Follow-Up Prior to IOP
☒ Confirm with Patient that you will follow-up on the Thursday or Friday prior to their arrival for IOP.

Final
Notes and Follow-up logistics:
No other issues.

Handout 13
Example of Blank PE- IOP Treatment Plan & Admission Review Checklist

(Modify for program specifics)[6]

Patient Information

Name:		Date	
IOP Start Date:			

Chart Review (before calling patient)

Phone Number:		Email	
Address:			Local Waitlist? ☐ YES ☐ NO
MRN:		Last 4:	

Psychiatric Diagnosis:	☐ PTSD ☐ MDD ☐ Bipolar I or II ☐ GAD ☐ OCD ☐ Social Anxiety ☐ Alcohol Use ☐ Drug use ☐ TBI ☐ PDD ☐ PD ☐ Other_____
Medical Diagnosis:	
Alcohol/ Substance:	
Suicidal Ideation:	Provided Patient's Crisis Line: 1-800-273-8255 Press 1 ☐ YES ☐ NO Weapon? ☐ YES ☐ NO Gun Lock Provided ☐ YES ☐ NO Safety Plan ☐ YES ☐ NO Date:

[6] This Handout was created by Lindy Carbone, LCSW, and Megan Goodlin, LCSW. Used with permission.

Treatment Plan from Case Conference:

(From Multidisciplinary Case Conference)

track: _____			Other Recommendations/ Notes:
SUD Consult ☐ YES ☐ NO	Healthy Behaviors ☐ YES ☐ NO	UDS ☐ YES ☐ NO	UDS needed? ☐ Pre 9/11
Sleep Consult ☐ YES ☐ NO	Sleep Study ☐ YES ☐ NO	TRD ☐ YES ☐ NO	Flying ~ 2 weeks prior Driving ~ 1 week prior Date for UDS:
Acupuncture ☐ Yes ☐ No		Massage ☐ Yes ☐ No ☐ M ☐ F ☐ Either	
Pers. Training ☐ Yes ☐ No		Ind. Pastor Session ☐ Yes ☐ No	
Anger Management ☐ YES ☐ NO			
Chronic Pain Group ☐ YES ☐ NO			
Neuropsych testing ☐ YES ☐ NO			
Smoking Cessation ☐ YES ☐ NO			
Research ☐ YES ☐ NO			
Home Treatment team needed? ☐ YES ☐ NO		Current therapist: Current PCP/ Psychiatrist:	DD214 received? ☐ YES ☐ NO

Program Checklist (Call Patient)

How would you like to be addressed while attending the program (e.g., first name, last name?)

Work/School Excuse Letter

Do you need any medical documentation for work or school for you to attend the IOP?

☐ YES   ☐ NO

Medication

Do you take medications?

☐ YES ☐ NO

If you take any medications, please be sure to bring all of your medications for the full 2 weeks.

☐ YES ☐ NO

Physical Health

Do you have any chronic health issues (for example, diabetes or sleep apnea), physical limitations, or mobility concerns (for example, do you use a cane, walker, or wheelchair)?

☐ YES ☐ NO

If YES, What are those issues or concerns and plan to address those concerns?

Service Dog

Do you have a service animal? ☐ YES ☐ NO

Review service animal and relevant program requirements

Legal Needs

Do you have any ongoing legal issues that you would have to attend to while you are in our program (for example, family court, traffic court, or recent arrests)?

☐ YES ☐ NO

If yes, what are those issues?

Personal Needs

Do you have any housing or other immediate needs that need to be addressed before coming to IOP?

☐ YES ☐ NO

If yes, what are those issues?

Dietary

Dietary restrictions or food allergies?

☐ YES ☐ NO

Note Allergy Details:

Determine Patient Communication Needs

Do you have a smartphone or tablet with reliable access to internet? ☐ YES   ☐ NO

Explain:

If yes, we will need you to be sure to bring it with you because there are apps that we have you download for the program. If no, then we will provide a recorder for individual sessions.

Rules/Guidelines for IOP

Participation in the IOP is subject to the observance of the organization's rules and procedures. The activities that I am about to outline are strictly prohibited. Any patient who violates this Code is subject to removal from the program.

- *No abusive, rude, and/or disrespectful language toward a staff member, volunteer, or another patient.*
- *Do not use or bring drugs or alcohol to the program, including during travel to and from the program. We do random breathalyzer and drug screens, and a positive result will result in a discussion with your treatment team and could also result in you being sent home early.*
- *Do not bring dangerous or unauthorized materials such as explosives, firearms, or other weapons.*
- *No sexual contact with another patient and no sexual or gender-based harassment of a fellow patient, staff member, or volunteer will be tolerated.*
- *Actual or threatened violence or harm toward yourself, any other individual, or group members will not be tolerated.*

  Do you agree to follow these rules and guidelines?
  ☐ YES   ☐ NO
  Do you have any questions?
  ☐ YES   ☐ NO

Review Treatment Plan with Patient
Required:

☐ Wellness Program: sleep education, mindfulness, meeting with an individual wellness provider, and trauma-focused gentle yoga	☐ Finance and Careers: A class to learn about career and financial opportunities ☐ Weekend Activity: Explain that there is a weekend activity on either Saturday or Sunday

Family Therapy

This is a family skills group that provides psychoeducation about PTSD as well as skills to foster resilience.

Would you like a family member to be involved in these sessions via telehealth?

☐ YES ☐ NO

If NO, explain that patient can still participate in family sessions as an individual.

If YES, the family member is a: ☐ Spouse/Partner ☐ Parent ☐ Adult Child ☐ Other
Name and contact number of the Family Member:

Lodging:

Transportation:
Is the patient flying or driving? ☐ Needs Flight ☐ Driving

Flying:

Driving:

Follow-Up Prior to IOP
☐ Confirm with Patient that you will follow-up on the Thursday or Friday prior to their arrival for IOP.

Final

Notes and Follow-up logistics:

Handout 14
Example of Completed PE-IOP Goal Sheet

Name: John Doe[7]	
Start date of IOP: 10/21/2019	Graduation date of IOP: 11/01/2019
Therapist: Dr. Robbins	Case Manager: Ms. Gant
First Week	
Goals: (What do you hope to accomplish in the Intensive Outpatient Program?)	
*Reduce the nightmares and sleep more restfully *Be able to enjoy my family and not be angry all the time *Be able to think about my military career without anger and hate	
Strengths for achieving your goals:	Challenges to achieving your goals:
*Healthy person *Want things to change *Enjoy working a group	*Get angry easily and regret what I say *Wife is ready to leave *Job is in jeopardy due to "acting out" verbally
Second Week	
Achievements and Accomplishments:	
*Work on relationship with wife *Continue to approach the memory during in vivo and imaginal exposures	
Goals and Objectives at Discharge:	
*Maintain gains by continuing to approach in vivo situations working with Dr. Jyn *Consider additional couples counseling with wife *Begin attending yoga at the local facility	

---

[7] This Handout was created by Elizabeth Carbone, LCSW. Used with permission.

BRIEF CASE MANAGEMENT NEEDS ASSESSMENT

Do you currently have needs regarding any of the following? Add to list, if needed.

Resources	Notes	Check box (if needed)
Housing/food/clothing (basic life needs)	Stable	
Transportation needs	Stable	
Employment/education needs	Stable	
Childcare needs	Needed for the family session times	X
Family or relationship concerns	Wife sent him as last chance to reconcile	X
Medical needs	Stable	
Substance use concerns	None	
VA benefits	No need	
Financial concerns	Stable	
Legal concerns	Stable	

May I assist you with finding resources for any of the following? Add to list, if needed.

Religious or spiritual activities	Wants to reconnect with his Lutheran faith	
Recreational activities	Wants to get back into softball	
Support network/groups	Not enough time	
Additional mental health treatment		
Additional medical health treatment	Continue medications	
Family or relationship counseling	Reassess after return home	

NOTES:

Handout 15
Example of Blank PE-IOP Goal Sheet

Name:[8]	
Start date of IOP:	Graduation date of IOP:
Therapist:	Case Manager:
First Week	
Goals: (What do you hope to accomplish in the Intensive Outpatient Program?)	
Strengths for achieving your goals:	Challenges to achieving your goals:
Second Week	
Achievements and Accomplishments:	
Goals and Objectives at Discharge:	

---

[8] This Handout was created by Elizabeth Carbone, LCSW. Used with permission.

BRIEF CASE MANAGEMENT NEEDS ASSESSMENT

Do you currently have needs regarding any of the following? Add to list, if needed.

Resources	Notes	Check box (if needed)
Housing/food/clothing (basic life needs)		
Transportation needs		
Employment/education needs		
Childcare needs		
Family or relationship concerns		
Medical needs		
Substance use concerns		
VA benefits		
Financial concerns		
Legal concerns		

May I assist you with finding resources for any of the following? Add to list, if needed.

Religious or spiritual activities		
Recreational activities		
Support network/groups		
Additional mental health treatment		
Additional medical health treatment		
Family or relationship counseling		

NOTES:

Handout 16
Example of Completed PE-IOP Discharge Plan

<u>Mr. John Doe</u> has completed treatment for the 2-week Intensive Outpatient Program (IOP), designed to decrease the severity and improve the management of symptoms of posttraumatic stress and other trauma-related concerns.[9]

During the course of 2 weeks of treatment, the patient participated in individual therapy, group therapy, and pharmacotherapy (if needed). Additionally, the patient participated in a range of wellness activities that may have included: trauma sensitive yoga, mindfulness, acupuncture, massage, personal training, medication education, substance use, family/relationship psychoeducation, sleep education, anger management, and chronic pain management. A summary of the patient's progress in groups, individual therapy, and pharmacotherapy (if applicable) is described below followed by a description of discharge referrals arranged during course of treatment in the IOP.

Dates of Service:

10/21/2019   to   11/01/2019

Diagnosis at Intake:
- PTSD, chronic
- Major depressive disorder, recurrent

Current Risk Assessment:
- Suicidal Ideation/Homicide Ideation (SI/HI): Patient has denied any SI/HI during the course of this program, and no concerns have been noted/observed by clinical team.
- Mitigating factors: Patient has future-oriented goals, connection to treatment resources, effective problem-solving skills, insight, and care for self.

Current Symptoms:
- Thought: Clear, Coherent
- Behavior: Patient exhibited active engagement in all aspects of the program and positive goal focused orientation throughout
- Sleep issues: Patient participated in a Sleep Education class to learn healthy sleep hygiene

---

[9] This Handout was created by Elizabeth Carbone, LCSW; Danielle Wray, LCSW; and Giselle Remy-Bryan, MSW. Used with permission and with fake patient information.

- Appetite issues: Patient has reported no change overall with appetite
- Substance use: Patient has denied alcohol or substance use, and no concerns have been noted during course of the program

INDIVIDUAL PHARMACOTHERAPY

Patient recommended to continue on current medication regiment, no changes made during course of program. Patient should follow-up with PCP regarding medications and discuss current needs.

PROLONGED EXPOSURE THERAPY with Dr. Robbins

IN VIVO THERAPY with Dr. Raine and Dr. Karl

Recommendations:

Mr. Dane has progressed well through his target trauma memory and his symptoms related to that memory are no longer driving PTSD symptoms. He continues to avoid social connections and needs to continue to work on his in vivo hierarchy with Dr. Jyn. In addition to the work of in vivo, Mr. Dane will continue to expand his social network to maintain gains.

FAMILY SKILLS SESSIONS with Dr. Greene

CASE MANAGEMENT with Ms. Gant

Case management sessions focused on addressing the patient's goals for the program, logistics of program, and treatment/care coordination. Patient actively engaged in setting goals and participated in program planning to meet these needs. Encouraged the patient to continue to focus on overall wellness to support progress/gains from trauma-focused treatment and setting continued goals beyond treatment. Patient would likely benefit from continued engagement in treatment and following through with activities to address avoidance, which was discussed as part of ongoing treatment plan.

Case Manager's Recommendations: Patient is recommended to continue to re-explore hobbies and consider volunteer work in his local community. Patient is further recommended to attend all medical and mental health appointments with treatment providers and spend quality social time with supportive family and friends. Patient is encouraged to engage in activities with patient-oriented organizations.

WELLNESS SERVICES

Wellness Services focused on how to improve general function and health including:
- Nutrition and exercise
- Sleep
- Mindfulness
- Trauma sensitive yoga
- Acupuncture/massage/personal training
- Anger management, chronic pain group

INDIVIDUAL WELLNESS with Dr. Regan

Next Steps:
Continue with Mindful Movement twice weekly yoga at home and daily exercise plan.

Appointments/Referrals:
Patient to follow-up with local treatment team.

Appointments 11/7/19 at 10a Dr. Jyn at Hometown VA	Providers and Care Manager

1. Recommendations for post-IOP discharge
   Mr. Dane will reduce frequency of meetings with his treatment team as long as he continues to maintain his gains.

2. Patient is referred for individual/family therapy:

Facility N/A	

Resources:
Wounded Warrior Project
https://www.woundedwarriorproject.org/
Will assist with resources (financial, patient benefits, retreats, wellness, etc.)
Call the Resource Center at 888-WWP-ALUM (997-2586) or 904-405-1213

Local Vet Centers

https://www.vetcenter.va.gov/

For individual therapy or family therapy, if needed.

1-877-WAR-VETS Call Center

Outward Bound for Veterans

https://www.outwardbound.org/veteran-adventures/outward-bound-for-veterans/

Free outdoor adventure program for veterans

CAMO Challenge Aspen

https://challengeaspen.org/military/

Free outdoor adventure program for veterans; may include families

Veterans of Foreign Wars

https://www.vfw.org/assistance/financial-grants

Veteran's benefits assistance and financial assistance (if needed)

Semper Fi Fund

http://semperfifund.org/

Financial assistance (if needed)

Team RWB

https://www.teamrwb.org/

For volunteer and physical activity opportunities with veterans

211 Helpline Center

http://www.helplinecenter.org/2-1-1-community-resources/what-is-211/

Dial 211 on phone

Will connect with local program to help with resources in all areas including mental health, financial, and housing

For further care coordination, please contact Ms. Gant **at** 777-777-7777 .

Email: _gant@email.xxxxx____.

Overall, patient has been open to education and recommendations throughout the course of intensive treatment, appearing to benefit from the treatment, new skills, and education. Patient will likely benefit from additional follow-up with clinical services with care team locally to maintain the gains.

Suicide Crisis Line
1-800-273-8255
Hit 1 for Veterans Crisis Line
Text: 838255
Chat: www.VeteransCrisisLine.net

Handout 17
Example of Blank PE-IOP Discharge Plan

_____ has completed treatment for the 2-week Intensive Outpatient Program (IOP), designed to decrease the severity and improve the management of symptoms of posttraumatic stress and other trauma-related concerns.[10]

During the course of 2 weeks of treatment, _____ participated in individual therapy, group therapy, and pharmacotherapy (if needed). Additionally, _____ participated in a range of wellness activities that may have included: trauma sensitive yoga, mindfulness, acupuncture, massage, personal training, medication education, substance use, family/relationship psychoeducation, sleep education, anger management, and chronic pain management. A summary of _____'s progress in groups, individual therapy, and pharmacotherapy (if applicable) is described below followed by a description of discharge referrals arranged during course of treatment in the IOP.

<u>Dates of Service:</u> _____

_____

_____ to _____

<u>Diagnosis at Intake:</u>

▪

<u>Current Risk Assessment:</u>

▪ Suicidal Ideation/Homicide Ideation (SI/HI):
▪ Mitigating factors:

<u>Current Symptoms:</u>

▪ Thought:
▪ Behavior:
▪ Sleep issues:
▪ Appetite issues:
▪ Substance use:

---

[10] This Handout was created by Elizabeth Carbone, LCSW; Danielle Wray, LCSW; and Giselle Remy-Bryan, MSW. Used with permission.

INDIVIDUAL PHARMACOTHERAPY

PROLONGED EXPOSURE THERAPY with _____

IN VIVO THERAPY with _____

Recommendations:

FAMILY SKILLS SESSIONS with _____

CASE MANAGEMENT with _____

Case Manager's recommendations:

WELLNESS SERVICES

Wellness Services focused on how to improve general function and health including:

-
-

INDIVIDUAL WELLNESS with _____

Next Steps:

Appointments/referrals:

Appointments	Providers and Care Manager

1. Recommendations for post-IOP discharge

2. Patient is referred for individual/family therapy:

Facility	

Resources:

Wounded Warrior Project
https://www.woundedwarriorproject.org/
Will assist with resources (financial, patient benefits, retreats, wellness, etc.)
Call the Resource Center at 888-WWP-ALUM (997-2586) or 904-405-1213

Local Vet Centers
https://www.vetcenter.va.gov/
For individual therapy or family therapy, if needed.
1-877-WAR-VETS Call Center

Outward Bound for Veterans
https://www.outwardbound.org/veteran-adventures/outward-bound-for-veterans/
Free outdoor adventure program for veterans

CAMO Challenge Aspen
https://challengeaspen.org/military/
Free outdoor adventure program for veterans; may include families

Veterans of Foreign Wars
https://www.vfw.org/assistance/financial-grants
Veteran's benefits assistance and financial assistance (if needed)

Semper Fi Fund
http://semperfifund.org/
Financial assistance (if needed)

Team RWB
https://www.teamrwb.org/
For volunteer and physical activity opportunities with veterans

211 Helpline Center
http://www.helplinecenter.org/2-1-1-community-resources/what-is-211/
Dial 211 on phone
Will connect with local program to help with resources in all areas including mental health, financial, and housing

For further care coordination, please contact _____ at _____.
Email: _____.

Suicide Crisis Line

1-800-273-8255

Hit 1 for Veterans Crisis Line

Text: 838255

Chat: www.VeteransCrisisLine.net

PE-IOP Variation Handout

Handout 18
Breathing Retraining Technique

Purpose of Exercises[11]
- Slow down breathing
- Decrease amount of oxygen in blood
- With practice, decrease anxiety

Breathing Instructions

1. Take a normal breath in through your nose with your mouth closed.

2. Exhale slowly with your mouth closed.

3. On exhaling, silently say to yourself the word *calm* or *relax* very slowly; for example: *c-a-a-a-a-l-m* or *r-e-e-e-l-a-a-a-a-x*.

4. Pause, holding your breath, for a count of four, and then take the next inhalation.

5. Practice this exercise twice a day, for 10 minutes each time.

---

[11] This material originally was published as Handout 2 in *Reclaiming Your Life from a Traumatic Experience WORKBOOK* (2nd ed.) (Rothbaum et al., 2019). Reprinted by permission of Oxford University Press.

Intensive Outpatient Program Treatment Agreement

The EHVP Treatment program is dedicated to providing exceptional patient care in an environment that is safe and supportive for our patients and staff. In order to facilitate your treatment in the Intensive Outpatient Program (IOP), ensure that you and other patients are best supported in meeting your treatment goals, and maintain a secure and welcoming environment for all, we have several rules and guidelines for program participation. We ask that you carefully review the following Treatment Agreement outlining expectations for all program patients.

Your signature on this agreement indicates that you have read and fully understand all components of this agreement and that you will follow the terms in the agreement while you are in treatment. Your signature reflects your understanding that failure to abide by these terms may result in dismissal from the treatment program. If you have any questions about this agreement, please reach out to your case manager at any time prior to the IOP.

Case Manager Name:
Contact:
Your case manager will be your central contact for communication prior to and during the IOP. He or she will be able to assist you with any clinical or logistical needs you may have as related to your treatment plan. Please keep your case manager up to date with any health, legal, or logistical concerns that may impede your receiving care.

Personal Conduct

We all deserve to work on our mental health goals in an environment in which we are treated with dignity and respect. It is imperative to create an atmosphere of trust, camaraderie, support, and encouragement. The EHVP is committed to creating such an environment because it brings out the full potential in each of us. Participation in the IOP is subject to and conditional upon your observance of the rules and procedures as outlined in this document and all other applicable facility policies.

The activities outlined below are strictly prohibited during enrollment in the IOP. Any patient who violates this Treatment Agreement is subject to dismissal from the program.

1. Abusive language toward a staff member, volunteer, or another patient
2. Using drugs or alcohol during the program, including during travel to and from the program
3. Using medications that were not prescribed to you or using more than was prescribed
4. Bringing dangerous or unauthorized materials such as explosives, firearms, or weapons
5. Being disrespectful or rude to a fellow patient, staff member, or volunteer
6. Verbal, physical, or any other type of harassment toward another patient, staff, or volunteer
7. Actual or threatened violence or harm toward self or any other individual or group
8. Conduct endangering the life, safety, health, or well-being of self or others
9. Failure to follow the policies or procedures of the IOP or the program
10. Bullying or taking unfair advantage of any patient, volunteer, or staff
11. Sexual activity with another patient, staff, or volunteer, or any other risky or unsafe sexual behavior during enrollment in the IOP
12. Repeated failure to complete program activities and practice exercises
13. Interfering with others completing program exercises

Treatment Overview and Expectations

The IOP is a 2-week program that includes group and individual sessions during regular business hours on Monday through Friday of each week in the program. Evening and weekend activities are included in the program and are important components of your participation. All patients are expected to fully participate in scheduled program activities, including wellness and recreational activities. Please discuss any concerns about your schedule with your case manager. Requests for changes to your schedule will be considered on an individual basis.

We use a multidisciplinary team-based approach to treatment to provide you with the best care possible. Our clinical team includes physicians, psychologists, social workers, advanced practice clinical nurse specialists, and other health professionals with expertise in PTSD, traumatic brain injury (TBI), depression, anxiety, substance misuse, and other invisible wounds.

Patients in the IOP may receive different services, depending on each individual's specific goals and treatment plan. Treatment plans are developed based on thorough assessment by a multidisciplinary team. However, there are some elements common across all therapy, and common expectations for all program patients:

- Therapy is goal-directed, meaning it will focus on addressing symptoms or helping you make specific life changes, rather than providing general support.
- Therapy involves regular therapeutic practice assignments outside of sessions. Completion of practice assignments is a critical part of your treatment.
- All treatment is voluntary and you may end treatment at any time. However, we ask that you notify us if you decide to stop treatment.
- Some of the most effective treatments for PTSD, TBI, depression, and anxiety involve interventions that may be uncomfortable, such as confronting difficult or previously avoided memories, emotions, and situations. Most people find this type of therapy helpful, but it can be difficult at times and there can be no guarantees of what you will experience. We will support you in taking difficult steps toward recovery, and we will strongly encourage you to challenge yourself throughout the IOP.
- Out of respect for your fellow patients and EHVP staff, please arrive on time for your sessions and remain for the duration of the scheduled session. If you need to take a brief break during a group session, please speak with the group leader and limit your absence from the session to less than 10 minutes.
- During the course of treatment in the IOP, the treatment team may determine that you are in need of services, including medical or psychiatric services, which cannot be provided at the program. This may include coordinating additional appointments during your time in IOP that may cause you to miss other scheduled activities. This may also include early completion of your treatment in the IOP and referral to outside programs or providers for additional services.

In addition to the above, we have additional details on behavior in the housing venue, alcohol and drug use, personal and property safety, medical illness, medications, weapons, cell phones, service animals, and dismissal from the program.

Appendix B

PE-IOP Session Checklists

Day 1 (Monday)

Group In Vivo Exposure Session 1 Checklist (2 Hours)

Materials Needed

- Dry erase or other device to record group discussion in real time (Smart Board, etc.)
- Binder with Session Handouts (see Appendix A in this guide: Handout 1: Rationale for Treatment by Prolonged Exposure, Handout 2: Subjective Units of Distress & In Vivo Exposure Hierarchy, Handout 3: Common Reactions to Trauma, and Handout 4: List of Things to Take Back)

Session Outline

- Review posttraumatic stress disorder (PTSD) symptoms (30 minutes) and treatment rationale with analogy (20 minutes)
- Create Subjective Units of Distress Scale (SUDS) (10 minutes)
- Create in vivo hierarchy (50 minutes)
- Assign homework (10 minutes)

Individual Imaginal Exposure Session 1 Checklist (90 Minutes)

Materials Needed

- Recording device (prolonged exposure [PE] coach, smartphone, or other digital recording method)
- Binder with Session Handouts (see Appendix A in this guide: Handout 15: Example of Blank PE-IOP Goal Sheet, and Handout 6: Imaginal Exposure Homework Recording Form)
- Handout 5: Therapist Imaginal Exposure Recording Form

Session Outline

- Present individual session goals and rationale for imaginal exposure (15 minutes)
- Present directions and conduct imaginal exposure (45 minutes) and processing (15 minutes)
- Assign homework (5 minutes)

Group In Vivo Exposure Session 2 Checklist (2 Hours)

Materials Needed

- Dry erase or other device to record group discussion in real time (Smart Board, etc.)
- Binder with Session Handouts (see Appendix A in this guide: Handout 2: Subjective Units of Distress & In Vivo Exposure Hierarchy, Handout 7: Gradual Exposure, and Handout 8: In Vivo Exposure Homework Recording Form)

Session Outline

- Review homework (10 minutes)
- Expand in vivo hierarchy (30 minutes)

- Select items and complete exposure exercise individually or in group (75 minutes)
- Assign homework (5 minutes)

Day 3 (Wednesday)

Individual Imaginal Exposure Session 2 Checklist (90 Minutes)

Materials Needed

- Devices (PE coach, smartphone, or other digital recording method)
- Binder with Session Handouts (see Appendix A in this guide: Handout 6: Imaginal Exposure Homework Recording Form)
- Handout 5: Therapist Imaginal Exposure Recording Form

Session Outline

- Review homework (10 minutes)
- Conduct imaginal exposure (60 minutes) and processing (15 minutes)
- Assign homework (5 minutes)

Day 3 (Wednesday)

Group In Vivo Exposure Session 3 Checklist (2 Hours)

Materials Needed

- Dry erase or other device to record group discussion in real time (Smart Board, etc.)
- Binder with Session Handouts (see Appendix A in this guide: Handout 8: In Vivo Exposure Homework Recording Form) and Handout 9: Safety Behaviors

Session Outline

▪ Review homework (10 minutes)
▪ Discuss safety behaviors and address avoidance during in vivo exposure (25 minutes)
▪ Plan and complete in vivo exposure (65 minutes)
▪ Assign homework (10 minutes)

Days 4 Through 8 (Thursday, Friday, Monday, Tuesday, Wednesday)

Individual Imaginal Exposure Sessions 3 Through 7 Checklist (90 Minutes)

Materials Needed

▪ Devices (PE coach, smartphone, or other digital recording method)
▪ Binder with Session Handouts (see Appendix A in this guide: Handout 6: Imaginal Exposure Homework Recording Form)
▪ Handout 5: Therapist Imaginal Exposure Recording Form

Session Outline

▪ Review homework (10 minutes)
▪ Conduct imaginal exposure (60 minutes) and processing (15 minutes)
▪ Assign homework (5 minutes)

Days 4 Through 8 (Thursday, Friday, Monday, Tuesday, Wednesday)

Group In Vivo Exposure Sessions 4 Through 8 Checklist (2 Hours)

Materials Needed

▪ Dry erase or other device to record group discussion in real time (Smart Board, etc.)
▪ Binder with Session Handouts (see Appendix A in this guide: Handout 8: In Vivo Exposure Homework Recording Form)

Session Outline

- Review homework (10 minutes)
- Address avoidance during in vivo exposure (10 minutes)
- Plan and complete in vivo exposure (95 minutes)
- Assign homework (5 minutes)

Day 9 (Thursday)

Individual Imaginal Exposure Session 8 Checklist
(90 Minutes)

Materials Needed

- Devices (PE coach, smartphone, or other digital recording method)
- Binder with Session Handouts (see Appendix A in this guide: Handout 6: Imaginal Exposure Homework Recording Form)
- Handout 5: Therapist Imaginal Exposure Recording Form

Session Outline

- Review homework (10 minutes)
- Conduct imaginal exposure (60 minutes) and processing (15 minutes)
- Assign homework (5 minutes)

Day 9 (Thursday)

Group In Vivo Exposure Session 9 Checklist (1 Hour)

Materials Needed

- Dry erase or other device to record group discussion in real time (Smart Board, etc.)
- Binder with Session Handouts (see Appendix A in this guide: Handout 2: Subjective Units of Distress & In Vivo Exposure Hierarchy; Handout 10: Relapse Prevention Skills; and Handout 11: Managing Stress)

Session Outline (Final Session 60 Minutes Only)

- Review homework (10 minutes)
- Review in vivo progress and items that need more work (25 minutes)
- Discuss relapse prevention (20 minutes)
- Farewells (5 minutes)

Day 10 (Friday)

Individual Imaginal Exposure Session 9 Checklist (90 Minutes)

Materials Needed

- Devices (PE coach, smartphone, or other digital recording method)
- Binder with Session Handouts (see Appendix A in this guide: Handout 6: Imaginal Exposure Homework Recording Form)
- Handout 5: Therapist Imaginal Exposure Recording Form

Session Outline

- Review homework (10 minutes)
- Conduct imaginal exposure (60 minutes) and processing (15 minutes)
- Assign homework (5 minutes)

References

American Psychiatric Association. (2013). *Diagnostic and statistical manual of mental disorders* (5th ed.). Washington, DC: American Psychiatric Press.

American Psychological Association. (2017). *Clinical practice guideline for the treatment of PTSD.* http://www.apa.org/ptsd-guideline/ptsd.pdf

Barlow, D. H., & Farchione, T. J. (2018). *Applications of the unified protocol for transdiagnostic treatment of emotional disorder.* New York: Oxford University Press.

Beidel, D. C., Frueh, B. C., Neer, S. M., Bowers, C. A., Trachik, B., Uhde, T. W., & Grubaugh, A. (2019). Trauma management therapy with virtual-reality augmented exposure therapy for combat-related PTSD: A randomized controlled trial. *Journal of Anxiety Disorders, 61,* 64–74. doi:https://doi.org/10.1016/j.janxdis.2017.08.005

Beidel, D. C., Frueh, B. C., Neer, S. M., & Lejuez, C. W. (2017). The efficacy of Trauma Management Therapy: A controlled pilot investigation of a three-week intensive outpatient program for combat-related PTSD. *Journal of Anxiety Disorders, 50,* 23–32. doi:10.1016/j.janxdis.2017.05.001

Beidel, D. C., Stout, J. W., Neer, S. M., Frueh, B. C., & Lejuez, C. (2017). An intensive outpatient treatment program for combat-related PTSD: Trauma Management Therapy. *Bulletin of the Menninger Clinic, 81*(2), 107–122. doi:10.1521/bumc.2017.81.2.107

Blevins, C. A., Weathers, F. W., Davis, M. T., Witte, T. K., & Domino, J. L. (2015). The Posttraumatic Stress Disorder Checklist for DSM-5 (PCL-5): Development and initial psychometric evaluation. *Journal of Traumatic Stress, 28*(6), 489–498. doi:10.1002/jts.22059

Blount, T. H., Cigrang, J. A., Foa, E. B., Ford, H. L., & Peterson, A. L. (2014). Intensive outpatient prolonged exposure for combat-related PTSD: A case study. *Cognitive and Behavioral Practice, 21*(1), 89–96. doi:10.1016/j.cbpra.2013.05.004

Cahill, S. P., Rauch, S. A., Hembree, E. A., & Foa, E. B. (2004). Effect of cognitive-behavioral treatments for PTSD on anger. In S. Taylor (Ed.), *Advances in the treatment of posttraumatic stress disorder: Cognitive-behavioral perspectives* (pp. 175–196). New York: Springer.

Cloitre, M., Courtois, C. A., Charuvastra, A., Carapezza, R., Stolbach, B. C., & Green, B. L. (2011). Treatment of complex PTSD: Results of the ISTSS expert clinician survey on best practices. *Journal of Trauma and Stress, 24*(6), 615–627. doi:10.1002/jts.20697

Cloitre, M., Garvert, D. W., Brewin, C. R., Bryant, R. A., & Maercker, A. (2013). Evidence for proposed ICD-11 PTSD and complex PTSD: A latent profile analysis. *European Journal of Psychotraumatology, 4*. doi:10.3402/ejpt.v4i0.20706

Craske, M. G., Kircanski, K., Zelikowsky, M., Mystkowski, J., Chowdhury, N., & Baker, A. (2008). Optimizing inhibitory learning during exposure therapy. *Behavioral Research and Therapy, 46*(1), 5–27. doi:10.1016/j.brat.2007.10.003

Cusack, K., Jonas, D. E., Forneris, C. A., Wines, C., Sonis, J., Middleton, J. C., . . . Gaynes, B. N. (2016). Psychological treatments for adults with posttraumatic stress disorder: A systematic review and meta-analysis. *Clinical Psycholy Review, 43*, 128–141. doi:10.1016/j.cpr.2015.10.003

De Jongh, A., Resick, P. A., Zoellner, L. A., van Minnen, A., Lee, C. W., Monson, C. M., . . . Bicanic, I. A. (2016). Critical analysis of the current treatment guidelines for complex PTSD in adults. *Depression and Anxiety, 33*(5), 359–369. doi:10.1002/da.22469

Feeny, N. C., Zoellner, L. A., & Foa, E. B. (2002).Treatment outcome for chronic PTSD among female assault victims with borderline personality characteristics: A preliminary examination. *Journal of Personality Disorders, 16*, 30–40. PMID 11881159, doi:10.1521/pedi.16.1.30.22555

First, M., Williams, J., Karg, R., & Spitzer, R. (2015). *Structured clinical interview for DSM-5: Research Version (SCID-5 for DSM-5, Research Version; SCID-5-RV)*. Arlington, VA: American Psychiatric Association.

Foa, E. B., Ehlers, A., Clark, D. M., Tolin, D. F., & Orsillo, S. M. (1999). The Posttraumatic Cognitions Inventory (PTCI): Development and validation. *Psychological Assessment, 11*(3), 303–314. doi:10.1037/1040-3590.11.3.303

Foa, E. B., Hembree, E. A., & Rothbaum, B. O. (2007). *Prolonged exposure therapy for PTSD: Therapist guide*. New York: Oxford University Press.

Foa, E. B., Hembree, E. A., Rothbaum, B. O., & Rauch, S. A. M. (2019). *Prolonged exposure therapy for PTSD: Emotional processing of traumatic experiences* (2nd ed.). New York: Oxford University Press.

Foa, E. B., Huppert, J. D., & Cahill, S. P. (2006). Emotional processing theory: An update. In B. O. Rothbaum (Ed.), *Pathological anxiety: Emotional processing in etiology and treatment* (pp. 3–24). New York: The Guilford Press.

Foa, E. B., Keane, T. M., Friedman, M. J., & Cohen, J. A. (2009). *Effective treatments for PTSD: Practice guidelines from the International Society for Traumatic Stress Studies* (2nd ed.). New York: Guilford Press.

Foa, E. B., & McLean, C. P. (2016). The efficacy of exposure therapy for anxiety-related disorders and its underlying mechanisms: The case of OCD and PTSD. *Annual Review of Clinical Psychology, 12*, 1–28. doi:10.1146/annurev-clinpsy-021815-093533

Foa, E. B., McLean, C. P., Zang, Y., Rosenfield, D., Yadin, E., Yarvis, J. S., . . . Peterson, A. L. (2018). Effect of prolonged exposure therapy delivered over 2 weeks vs 8 weeks vs present-centered therapy on PTSD symptom severity in military personnel: A randomized clinical trial. *JAMA, 319*(4), 354–364. doi:10.1001/jama.2017.21242

Foa, E. B., McLean, C. P., Zang, Y., Zhong, J., Powers, M. B., Kauffman, B. Y., . . . Knowles, K. (2016). Psychometric properties of the Posttraumatic Diagnostic Scale for DSM-5 (PDS-5). *Psychological Assessment, 28*(10), 1166–1171. doi:10.1037/pas0000258

Foa, E. B., McLean, C. P., Zang, Y., Zhong, J., Rauch, S., Porter, K., . . . Kauffman, B. Y. (2016). Psychometric properties of the Posttraumatic Stress Disorder Symptom Scale Interview for DSM-5 (PSSI-5). *Psychological Assessment, 28*(10), 1159–1165. doi:10.1037/pas0000259

Foa, E. B., & Rauch, S. A. (2004). Cognitive changes during prolonged exposure versus prolonged exposure plus cognitive restructuring in female assault survivors with posttraumatic stress disorder. *Journal of Consulting and Clinical Psychology, 72*(5), 879–884. doi:10.1037/0022-006x.72.5.879

Foa, E. B., Riggs, D. S., Massie, E. D., & Yarczower, M. (1995). The impact of fear activation and anger on the efficacy of exposure treatment for posttraumatic stress disorder. *Behavior Therapy, 26*(3), 487–499. doi:10.1016/S0005-7894(05)80096-6

Foa, E. B., Zoellner, L. A., Feeny, N. C., Hembree, E. A., & Alvarez-Conrad, J. (2002). Does imaginal exposure exacerbate PTSD symptoms? *Journal of Consulting and Clinical Psychology, 70*(4), 1022–1028. doi:10.1037//0022-006x.70.4.1022

Hagenaars, M. A., van Minnen, A., & Hoogduin, K. A. (2010). The impact of dissociation and depression on the efficacy of prolonged exposure treatment for PTSD. *Behaviour Research and Therapy, 48*(1), 19–27. doi:10.1016/j.brat.2009.09.001

Harned, M. S., Korslund, K. E., Foa, E. B., & Linehan, M. M. (2012). Treating PTSD in suicidal and self-injuring women with borderline personality disorder: Development and preliminary evaluation of a dialectical behavior therapy prolonged exposure protocol. *Behaviour Research and Therapy, 50*(6), 381–386. doi:10.1016/j.brat.2012.02.011

Harned, M. S., Korslund, K. E., & Linehan, M. M. (2014). A pilot randomized controlled trial of dialectical behavior therapy with and without the dialectical behavior therapy prolonged exposure protocol for suicidal and self-injuring women with borderline personality disorder and PTSD. *Behaviour Research and Therapy, 55*, 7–17. doi:10.1016/j.brat.2014.01.008

Harvey, M. M., Petersen, T. J., Sager, J. C., Makhija-Graham, N. J., Wright, E. C., Clark, E. L., . . . Simon, N. M. (2019). An intensive outpatient program for veterans with posttraumatic stress disorder and traumatic brain injury. *Cognitive and Behavioral Practice, 26*(2), 323–334. https://doi.org/10.1016/j.cbpra.2018.07.003

Harvey, M. M., Rauch, S. A. M., Zalta, A. K., Sornborger, J., Pollack, M. H., Rothbaum, B. O., . . . Simon, N. M. (2017). Intensive treatment models to address posttraumatic stress among post-9/11 warriors: The Warrior Care Network. *Focus, 15*(4), 378–383. doi:10.1176/appi.focus.20170022

Hembree, E. A., Cahill, S. P., & Foa, E. B. (2004). Impact of personality disorders on treatment outcome for female assault survivors with chronic posttraumatic stress disorder. *Journal of Personality Disorders, 18*(1), 117–127.

Hendriks, L., Kleine, R. A., Heyvaert, M., Becker, E. S., Hendriks, G. J., & Minnen, A. (2017). Intensive prolonged exposure treatment for adolescent complex posttraumatic stress disorder: A single-trial design. *Journal of Child Psychology and Psychiatry, 58*(11), 1229–1238. doi:10.1111/jcpp.12756

Hoge, C. W., Auchterlonie, J. L., & Milliken, C. S. (2006). Mental health problems, use of mental health services, and attrition from military service after returning from deployment to Iraq or Afghanistan. *JAMA, 295*(9), 1023–1032. doi:10.1001/jama.295.9.1023

Humphreys, L., Westerink, J., Giarratano, L., & Brooks, R. (1999). An intensive treatment program for chronic posttraumatic stress disorder: 2-year outcome data. *Australian and New Zealand Journal of Psychiatry, 33*(6), 848–854. doi:10.1046/j.1440-1614.1999.00640.x

Institute of Medicine (2008). *Treatment of posttraumatic stress disorder: An assessment of the evidence.* Washington, DC: The National Academies Press. https://doi.org/10.17226/11955.

Jaycox, L. H., Foa, E. B., & Morral, A. R. (1998). Influence of emotional engagement and habituation on exposure therapy for PTSD. *Journal of Consulting and Clinical Psychology, 66*(1), 185–192. doi:10.1037//0022-006x.66.1.185

Kleim, B., Grey, N., Wild, J., Nussbeck, F. W., Stott, R., Hackmann, A., . . . Ehlers, A. (2013). Cognitive change predicts symptom reduction with cognitive therapy for posttraumatic stress disorder. *Journal of Consulting and Clinical Psychology, 81*(3), 383–393. doi:10.1037/a0031290

Kroenke, K., Spitzer, R. L., & Williams, J. B. W. (2001). The PHQ-9: Validity of a Brief Depression Severity Measure. *Journal of General Internal Medicine, 16*, 606–613.

Kumpula, M. J., Pentel, K. Z., Foa, E. B., LeBlanc, N. J., Bui, E., McSweeney, L. B., . . . Rauch, S. A. (2017). Temporal sequencing of change in posttraumatic cognitions and PTSD symptom reduction during prolonged exposure therapy. *Behavior Therapy, 48*(2), 156–165. doi:10.1016/j.beth.2016.02.008

Lee, D. J., Schnitzlein, C. W., Wolf, J. P., Vythilingam, M., Rasmusson, A. M., & Hoge, C. W. (2016). Psychotherapy versus pharmacotherapy for posttraumatic stress disorder: Systemic review and meta-analyses to determine first-line treatments. *Depression and Anxiety, 33*(9), 792–806. doi:10.1002/da.22511

Lester, P., Mogil, C., Saltzman, W., Woodward, K., Nash, W., Leskin, G., . . . Beardslee, W. (2011). Families overcoming under stress: implementing family-centered prevention for military families facing wartime deployments and combat operational stress. *Mil Med, 176*(1), 19–25. doi:10.7205/milmed-d-10-00122

Mataix-Cols, D., Fernandez de la Cruz, L., Monzani, B., Rosenfield, D., Andersson, E., Perez-Vigil, A., . . . Thuras, P. (2017). D-cycloserine augmentation of exposure-based cognitive behavior therapy for anxiety, obsessive-compulsive, and posttraumatic stress disorders: A systematic review and meta-analysis of individual participant data. *JAMA Psychiatry, 74*(5), 501–510. doi:10.1001/jamapsychiatry.2016.3955

McLean, C. P., Su, Y.-J., & Foa, E. B. (2014). Posttraumatic stress disorder and alcohol dependence: Does order of onset make a difference? *Journal of Anxiety Disorders, 28*(8), 894–901. doi:10.1016/j.janxdis.2014.09.023

McLean, C. P., Yeh, R., Rosenfield, D., & Foa, E. B. (2015). Changes in negative cognitions mediate PTSD symptom reductions during client-centered therapy and prolonged exposure for adolescents. *Behaviour Research and Therapy, 68*, 64–69. doi:10.1016/j.brat.2015.03.008

Mithoefer, M. C., Wagner, M. T., Mithoefer, A. T., Jerome, L., & Doblin, R. (2011). The safety and efficacy of {+/–}3,4-methylenedioxymethamphetamine-assisted psychotherapy in subjects with chronic, treatment-resistant posttraumatic stress disorder: The first randomized controlled pilot study. *Journal of Psychopharmacology (Oxford, England), 25*(4), 439–452. doi:10.1177/0269881110378371

Moser, J. S., Hajcak, G., Simons, R. F., & Foa, E. B. (2007). Posttraumatic stress disorder symptoms in trauma-exposed college students: The role of trauma-related cognitions, gender, and negative affect. *Journal of Anxiety Disorders, 21*(8), 1039–1049. doi:10.1016/j.janxdis.2006.10.009

Nacasch, N., Huppert, J. D., Su, Y.-J., Kivity, Y., Dinshtein, Y., Yeh, R., & Foa, E. B. (2015). Are 60-minute prolonged exposure sessions with 20-minute imaginal exposure to traumatic memories sufficient to successfully treat

PTSD? A randomized noninferiority clinical trial. *Behavior Therapy, 46*(3), 328–341. doi:10.1016/j.beth.2014.12.002

Oprel, D. A. C., Hoeboer, C. M., Schoorl, M., De Kleine, R. A., Wigard, I. G., Cloitre, M., . . . Van der Does, W. (2018). Improving treatment for patients with childhood abuse related posttraumatic stress disorder (IMPACT study): Protocol for a multicenter randomized trial comparing prolonged exposure with intensified prolonged exposure and phase-based treatment. *BMC Psychiatry, 18*.

Pitman, R. K., Orr, S. P., Altman, B., Longpre, R. E., Poire, R. E., & Macklin, M. L. (1996). Emotional processing during eye movement desensitization and reprocessing therapy of Vietnam veterans with chronic posttraumatic stress disorder. *Comprehensive Psychiatry, 37*(6), 419–429. doi:10.1016/s0010-440x(96)90025-5

Pollack, M. H., Simon, N. M., & Rothbaum, B. O. (2017). Care of veterans through the Warrior Care Network. *Focus, 15*(4), 377. doi:10.1176/appi.focus.20170037

Rabinak, C. A., Angstadt, M., Lyons, M., Mori, S., Milad, M. R., Liberzon, I., & Phan, K. L. (2014). Cannabinoid modulation of prefrontal-limbic activation during fear extinction learning and recall in humans. *Neurobiology of Learning and Memory, 113*, 125–134. doi:10.1016/j.nlm.2013.09.009

Ragsdale, K. A., Neer, S. M., Beidel, D. C., Frueh, B. C., & Stout, J. W. (2013). Posttraumatic stress disorder in OEF/OIF veterans with and without traumatic brain injury. *Journal of Anxiety Disorders, 27*(4), 420–426. doi:10.1016/j.janxdis.2013.04.003

Ragsdale, K. A., Sprang, K., Nichols, A., Penna, S., Rauch, S., & Rothbaum, B. O. (2019). PTSD complicated by history of mTBI can be effectively treated within a two-week intensive outpatient treatment program. Poster presented at the Association for Behavior and Cognitive Therapy annual meeting, Atlanta, GA.

Ragsdale, K. A., & Voss Horrell, S. C. (2016). Effectiveness of prolonged exposure and cognitive processing therapy for U.S. Veterans with a history of traumatic brain injury. *Journal of Traumatic Stress, 29*(5), 474–477. doi:10.1002/jts.22130

Rauch, S. A. M., Foa, E. B., Furr, J. M., & Filip, J. C. (2004). Imagery vividness and perceived anxious arousal in prolonged exposure treatment for PTSD. *Journal of Traumatic Stress, 17*(6), 461–465. doi:10.1007/s10960-004-5794-8

Rauch, S. A. M., King, A. P., Abelson, J., Tuerk, P. W., Smith, E., Rothbaum, B. O., . . . Liberzon, I. (2015). Biological and symptom changes in posttraumatic stress disorder treatment: A randomized clinical trial. *Depression and Anxiety, 32*(3), 204–212. doi:10.1002/da.22331

Rauch, S. A. M., Yasinski, C. W., Post, L. M., Jovanovic, T. J., Norrholm, S. N., Sherrill, A. M., . . . Rothbaum, B. O. (in press). An intensive outpatient program with prolonged exposure for veterans with posttraumatic stress disorder: Retention, predictors, and patterns of change. *Psychological Services.*

Resick, P. A., Bovin, M. J., Calloway, A. L., Dick, A. M., King, M. W., Mitchell, K. S., . . . Wolf, E. J. (2012). A critical evaluation of the complex PTSD literature: Implications for DSM-5. *Journal of Traumatic Stress, 25*(3), 241–251. doi:10.1002/jts.21699

Rothbaum, B. O., Foa, E. B., Hembree, E. A., & Rauch, S. A. M. (2019). *Reclaiming your life from a traumatic experience: A prolonged exposure treatment program: Workbook* (2nd ed.). New York: Oxford University Press.

Rothbaum, B. O., Price, M., Jovanovic, T., Norrholm, S. D., Gerardi, M., Dunlop, B., . . . Ressler, K. J. (2014). A randomized, double-blind evaluation of D-cycloserine or alprazolam combined with virtual reality exposure therapy for posttraumatic stress disorder in Iraq and Afghanistan War veterans. *American Journal of Psychiatry, 171*(6), 640–648. doi:10.1176/appi.ajp.2014.13121625

Smith, E. R., Duax, J. M., & Rauch, S. A. M. (2013). Perceived perpetration during traumatic events: Clinical suggestions from experts in prolonged exposure therapy. *Cognitive and Behavioral Practice, 20*(4), 461–470. doi:10.1016/j.cbpra.2012.12.002

Smith, E. R., Porter, K. E., Messina, M. G., Beyer, J. A., Defever, M. E., Foa, E. B., & Rauch, S. A. (2015). Prolonged exposure for PTSD in a veteran group: A pilot effectiveness study. *Journal of Anxiety Disorders, 30*, 23–27.

Sripada, R. K., & Rauch, S. A. (2015). Between-session and within-session habituation in Prolonged Exposure Therapy for posttraumatic stress disorder: A hierarchical linear modeling approach. *Journal of Anxiety Disorders, 30*, 81–87. doi:10.1016/j.janxdis.2015.01.002

Sripada, R. K., Rauch, S. A., Tuerk, P. W., Smith, E., Defever, A. M., Mayer, R. A., . . . Venners, M. (2013). Mild traumatic brain injury and treatment response in prolonged exposure for PTSD. *Journal of Traumatic Stress, 26*(3), 369–375.

Tolin, D. F., Gilliam, C., Wootton, B. M., Bowe, W., Bragdon, L. B., Davis, E., . . . Hallion, L. S. (2018). Psychometric properties of a structured diagnostic interview for DSM-5 anxiety, mood, and obsessive-compulsive and related disorders. *Assessment, 25*(1), 3–13. doi:10.1177/1073191116638410

Tuerk, P. W., Yoder, M., Grubaugh, A., Myrick, H., Hamner, M., & Acierno, R. (2011). Prolonged exposure therapy for combat-related posttraumatic stress disorder: An examination of treatment effectiveness for veterans of the wars in Afghanistan and Iraq. *Journal of Anxiety Disorders, 25*(3), 397–403. doi:10.1016/j.janxdis.2010.11.002

VA/DOD. (2017). *Veterans Affairs and Department of Defense clinical practice guideline for the management of post-traumatic stress.* Retrieved from https://www.healthquality.va.gov/guidelines/MH/ptsd/VADoDPTSDCPGFinal012418.pdf

van Minnen, A., & Foa, E. B. (2006). The effect of imaginal exposure length on outcome of treatment for PTSD. *Journal of Traumatic Stress, 19*(4), 427–438. doi:10.1002/jts.20146

van Minnen, A., & Hagenaars, M. (2002). Fear activation and habituation patterns as early process predictors of response to prolonged exposure treatment in PTSD. *Journal of Traumatic Stress, 15*(5), 359–367. doi:10.1023/a:1020177023209

van Minnen, A., Harned, M. S., Zoellner, L., & Mills, K. (2012). Examining potential contraindications for prolonged exposure therapy for PTSD. *European Journal of Psychotraumatology, 3.* doi:10.3402/ejpt.v3i0.18805

Van Woudenberg, C., Voorendonk, E. M., Bongaerts, H., Zoet, H. A., Verhagen, M., Lee, C. W., . . . De Jongh, A. (2018). Effectiveness of an intensive treatment programme combining prolonged exposure and eye movement desensitization and reprocessing for severe post-traumatic stress disorder. *European Journal of Psychotraumatology, 9*(1). doi:10.1080/20008198.2018.1487225

Watts, B. V., Schnurr, P. P., Mayo, L., Young-Xu, Y., Weeks, W. B., & Friedman, M. J. (2013). Meta-analysis of the efficacy of treatments for posttraumatic stress disorder. *Journal of Clinical Psychiatry, 74*(6), e541–550. doi:10.4088/JCP.12r08225

Weathers, F. W., Bovin, M. J., Lee, D. J., Sloan, D. M., Schnurr, P. P., Kaloupek, D. G., . . . Marx, B. P. (2018). The clinician-administered PTSD Scale for DSM–5 (CAPS-5): Development and initial psychometric evaluation in military veterans. *Psychological Assessment, 30*(3), 383–395. doi:10.1037/pas0000486

Wolf, G. K., Kretzmer, T., Crawford, E., Thors, C., Wagner, H. R., Strom, T. Q., . . . Vanderploeg, R. D. (2015). Prolonged exposure therapy with veterans and active duty personnel diagnosed with PTSD and traumatic brain injury. *Journal of Traumatic Stress, 28*(4), 339–347. doi:10.1002/jts.22029

Yasinski, C., Sherrill, A. M., Maples-Keller, J. L., Rauch, S. A. M., & Rothbaum, B. O. (2018). Intensive outpatient prolonged exposure for PTSD in post 9-11 veterans and service members: Program structure and preliminary outcomes of the Emory Healthcare Veterans Program. *Trauma Psychology News, 12*(3), 1–3.

Zalta, A. K., Gillihan, S. J., Fisher, A. J., Mintz, J., McLean, C. P., Yehuda, R., & Foa, E. B. (2014). Change in negative cognitions associated with PTSD predicts symptom reduction in prolonged exposure. *Journal of Consulting and Clinical Psychology, 82*(1), 171–175. doi:10.1037/a0034735

Zoellner, L. A., Telch, M., Foa, E. B., Farach, F. J., McLean, C. P., Gallop, R., . . . Gonzalez-Lima, F. (2017). Enhancing extinction learning in posttraumatic stress disorder with brief daily imaginal exposure and methylene blue: A randomized controlled trial. *Journal of Clinical Psychiatry, 78*(7), e782–e789. doi:10.4088/JCP.16m10936

Zoet, H. A., Wagenmans, A., van Minnen, A., & de Jongh, A. (2018). Presence of the dissociative subtype of PTSD does not moderate the outcome of intensive trauma-focused treatment for PTSD. *European Journal of Psychotraumatology, 9*(1). doi:10.1080/20008198.2018.1468707

Sheila A. M. Rauch, PhD, ABPP, is the Mark and Barbara Klein Distinguished Professor in Psychiatry in the Department of Psychiatry and Behavioral Sciences at the Emory University School of Medicine. She serves as Deputy Director of the Emory Healthcare Veterans Program and Director of Mental Health Research and Program Evaluation at the VA Atlanta Healthcare System. Dr. Rauch received her degree from the University of North Dakota in 2000. She has been conducting research and providing posttraumatic stress disorder (PTSD) and anxiety disorders treatment for more than 20 years. Her research focuses on examination of biological and psychological mechanisms involved in the development and treatment of PTSD and improving access to effective interventions. She has been training providers in PTSD treatment since 2000. She has published scholarly articles and book chapters in the areas of anxiety disorders and PTSD, focusing on neurobiology and factors involved in the development, maintenance, and treatment of anxiety disorders, psychosocial factors in medical settings, and the relation between physical health and anxiety. Dr. Rauch has been involved in the modification and adaptation of proven psychotherapeutic interventions for anxiety disorders for various populations and settings, including primary care. She holds a diplomate in cognitive and behavioral psychology, is a fellow of the Association of Behavioral and Cognitive Therapy (ABCT), and a member of the Board of Directors and Scientific Council of the Anxiety and Depression Association of America.

Barbara O. Rothbaum, PhD, is Director of the Emory Healthcare Veterans Program. She is a professor and Associate Vice Chair of Clinical Research at Emory School of Medicine in the Department of Psychiatry and Behavioral Sciences and Director of the Trauma and Anxiety Recovery Program; she holds the Paul A. Janssen Chair in Neuropsychopharmcology. Dr. Rothbaum specializes in research on the treatment of anxiety disorders, particularly PTSD. Dr. Rothbaum has been studying PTSD treatments since 1986 and has developed, tested, and disseminated some of the most innovative and effective treatments available for PTSD. She is an inventor of virtual reality exposure therapy. She was a pioneer in applying it in the treatment of PTSD in combat veterans. She has authored more than 350 scientific papers and chapters, has published 11 books on the treatment of PTSD and edited 4 others on anxiety, and received the Diplomate in Behavioral Psychology from the American Board of Professional Psychology. She is a past president of the International Society of Traumatic Stress Studies (ISTSS), and is a fellow of the American College of Neuropsychopharmacology (ACNP), the National Academy of Inventors (NAI), the Association for Behavioral and Cognitive Therapies (ABCT), and American Psychological Association's Division 56 (Division of Trauma Psychology), and she was awarded the 2010 Award for Outstanding Contributions to the Practice of Trauma Psychology for APA Division 56 and the Robert S. Laufer Award for Outstanding Scientific Achievement from the International Society for Traumatic Stress Studies (ISTSS). Her outreach efforts include training community clinicians in evidence-based treatment for PTSD.

Erin R. Smith, PhD, is a staff psychologist at the VA Ann Arbor Healthcare System and Clinical Assistant Professor in the Department of Psychiatry, University of Michigan Medical School. She serves in administrative, supervisory, and clinical roles within the VA Ann Arbor Healthcare System. Dr. Smith received her degree from Fuller Theological Seminary, Graduate School of Psychology, in 2007. She has been providing clinical interventions for veterans with PTSD within the VA system for the past 14 years. She has been involved in research that focuses on improving access to effective interventions and the impact of comorbidity and type of trauma exposure on the development and trajectory of PTSD symptoms. Dr. Smith has been involved in the training and consultation of VA providers in prolonged exposure therapy since 2010. She has published scholarly articles and book chapters related to PTSD, comorbidity issues, trauma type, and the influence of traumatic brain injury.

Edna B. Foa, PhD, is a Professor of Psychiatry at the University of Pennsylvania and Founding Director of the Center for the Treatment and

Study of Anxiety in the Perelman School of Medicine, at the University of Pennsylvania. Dr. Foa has devoted her academic career to studying the psychopathology and treatment of anxiety and related disorders, primarily PTSD and obsessive-compulsive disorder (OCD). The treatment program she developed for PTSD has received the highest evidence for its efficacy and has been widely disseminated in the United States and around the world.